EXPLORATIONS IN WORSHIP

EXPLORATIONS IN WORSHIP

by
SHEILA M. HOBDEN

Thirty-five Services
for
Senior School Assembly

LUTTERWORTH EDUCATIONAL
GUILDFORD AND LONDON

First published 1970
Second impression 1972
Third impression 1974
Fourth impression 1977

Lutterworth Educational, Guildford and London

ISBN 0 7188 1549 1

Printed in Great Britain
by Ebenezer Baylis and Son Ltd.
The Trinity Press, Worcester, and London

Contents

Acknowledgements

The author and publisher acknowledge the willing help and co-operation of all those who have supplied information or given permission for their material to be used. A list of such sources is to be found after each section.

Introduction

PRAYERS TO MAKE YOU THINK

'INSTEAD OF THE OLD, incomprehensible prayers we want more, newer prayers concerning subjects of our time, in naturally phrased language which will make people think.'

This remark made by a fourteen year old is not without significance. 'Prayers to make people think' may not seem to some to be a proper understanding of prayer, but so much does it reveal about the way of thinking of secondary pupils about assembly that we should be foolish to dismiss the idea too hastily and without giving some thought to certain basic ideas underlying the act of worship in schools.

Various writers have offered their own definitions of worship, and perhaps one of the most embracing is Nels Ferre's comment that in worship we behold the goodness of God and become partakers of that goodness, we see the patience of God and become possessed by it, we glimpse the purpose of God and enlist in it, we meet the power of God and stand in its strengthening. This definition speaks of worship as a two-way activity. It brings vividly before the worshipper the dimension of depth in the object of worship: it makes God more real. And it enhances the quality of his response, by deepening his sense of awe or of need, by suggesting ways in which his desire to give himself more fully may be translated into forms of action which embrace his relationship not only to his God, but also to his fellow men. The British Council of Churches report, *Religion and the Secondary School* (Colin Alves, S.C.M. Press), speaking more particularly of the school situation, affirmed that 'school assembly is not to be thought of merely as a time of self offering, a declaration of commitment by the committed—though it is that—but also as an educative instrument, a means to insight, an evocation of vision'.

A partial description of worship, in perhaps rather simpler terms, is that it is an opportunity to respond to the deepest in one's self, to one's friends, to beauty, to life or to God. There is no significance in this order and it is understood that God is in one's friends, beauty or life. Sometimes this response will be in the form of an acknowledgement, sometimes an inner rejoicing or happiness, sometimes in a fresh conviction that there is more to life or in a saying that one had seen before, sometimes the expression of doubt or the formulation of a question about life, and perhaps very occasionally it will be in the form of an offering of the self in such an act as has traditionally been described by the word dedication.

The task of the leader of worship in schools is to create a situation to enable the pupil to make an offering in his own way, and so grow a little more into the fullness of a human person. How can this be done?

Before moving on to be specifically practical we must think carefully about the people involved in school worship. In spite of all the discussions about child centred education and the necessity of relevance, it is still necessary to assert that the act of worship must have meaning for the child. One still hears prayers and Bible readings used that can only have been chosen for the staff and served to confirm the child in his belief that religion is unintelligible and irrelevant. Any reading from any source is given credence by the child if it has meaning within his own experience. The Bible is not the 'Holy Bible' because of a theory about it, but because experience confirms it. The belief that the Bible has authority is one which will grow only at the rate of the child's own experience of its significance.

This means that before we can prepare an act of worship we must have probed the child's experience at depth for meaning. The worship will then be planned within the life experience of the children, even though we may feel that the experience is incomplete. C. Day Lewis tells us in his autobiography[1], 'it was not then because chapel was compulsory and Christianity an arm of the establishment that boys cultivated a resistance or an indifference to religion, so much as because in the form it was presented to us it seemed ill-related with life as we knew it, and evasive —and sometimes dishonest—about our own problems'. So, the life of the child or adolescent, his social and home background, his psychological, physical and educational development, the international scene as it impinges on him—these are the beginning points of worship. Because of this the teachers might find no satisfaction in the worship, but the worship of the school is not for them.

The basic assertion here is then that the child or adolescent is a major source of worship material. The second major resource is the school; this means the teachers and whole classes and the varied skills and facilities represented there.

All this argues that a great deal of hard thinking and hard work needs to be devoted to the subject of school worship. May be the production of a book of assembly services is not the best way to meet the problem! It is evident from the correspondence and conversations which I have had with a number of teachers that many are much concerned with this question. They feel that the problem is not simply that of finding suitable modern readings, but much more a question of the whole approach and form of assembly. The experimental school assemblies produced by the Christian Education Movement have been warmly received in schools, not only because of the contemporary material contained in them, but perhaps more so because they have suggested a greater variety in approach.

[1] *The Buried Day*. Chatto and Windus.

It is recognized that more experimental assembly services raise practical problems in the school. Some of these are of course more difficult to overcome than others; clearly, a school anxious to produce lively and stimulating school worship would need to give some thought to the assembly well before the event. Thought should be given in advance to the content of the assembly, the use of visual aid material and the participation of the pupils. In this particular set of suggested assembly services, from time to time visual aid material is referred to and this should be noted in advance. Furthermore prayers in response form might be duplicated in advance so that all members of the school can participate fully at this point. Even the arrangement of the hall may vary from day to day. It is often true that the arrangement of chairs in the hall in a semicircular setting is more conducive to a corporate atmosphere than straight rows of chairs facing the platform.

In this collection of assemblies, sometimes 'readers' are referred to and sometimes 'voices'. 'Readers' in most cases refers to a straightforward reading of part of the assembly, and the numbers point out when it would be advantageous to have a change of reader. Where a 'voice' is suggested, this indicates a new group of readers other than any other readers suggested in that assembly. The people taking the part of the voices could be in a separate group in a central place in the assembly or they could be voices coming from various parts of the hall where the assembly is taking place.

In spite of the extra work involved in preparation I am convinced that we must be ready to experiment as widely as possible in order to produce worship which is real for young people and to which they can respond. This means using drama, mime, silence, film and other audio and visual materials as much as possible, and wherever possible using material prepared by the young people themselves.

One further difficulty which arises in the school situation is that of the very wide age range between the youngest and the oldest pupils. Many schools have found that much has been gained by dividing the school and so providing material more suited to the age of those present. The same difficulty occurs in trying to prepare a collection of assembly services and these assemblies have been prepared with the average fourteen year old in mind.

All biblical references refer to the New English Bible in the case of the New Testament and the Revised Standard Version in the case of the Old Testament unless otherwise stated.

These assembly services are merely suggestions and it is hoped that they will lead the schools onward to prepare their own acts of worship for their own communities. Perhaps in doing so, we shall discover that the adolescent who asked for prayers to 'make people think' will be found to be rather nearer to the heart of worship than we had suspected.

SHEILA M. HOBDEN

9

1 MY WORLD

(a) Families

Song   Thank you, verses 1–4.

Reader 1 **The Family Together.**
  The day before we go on our holidays
  Everyone is packing up their things,
  My father finds the railway tickets
  Which he had bought some weeks before.

  Everyone is very excited,
  And soon the packing is done.
  All the cases are brought downstairs
  Ready for the time of departure.

  Soon it is time to go to bed
  Everyone's dreaming of their holidays,
  But soon the day of departure arrives
  And everyone is ready on time.

  To the station we travel
  My mother and father and I,
  And on the train we get
  Accompanied by our excitement.

Reader 2 **A Family Re-union.**
  Excitement was inside me as I walked into the house
  Joy and excitement in every one's heart and soul,
  My brother home at last
  For the first time in nearly two years.
  To see him again was so wonderful.
  As I ran over to him I felt tears for joy in my eyes.
  Then I ran over to him.

Everyone was happy and excited, but as I thought my happiness went,
One of the family was happy, but not with us to share our excitement.
In a moment the excitement and all the noise was over,
But all still very happy.

Reader 3 **A Family Celebrate.**

From *A Christmas Carol*, the Cratchit family celebrate Christmas. The family consisted of Bob and Mrs. Cratchit, Peter, Martha, Belinda, two younger Cratchits and Tiny Tim, the delicate cripple boy. They were not a handsome family; they were not well-dressed; their shoes were far from being water-proof; their clothes were scanty; and Peter might have known, and very likely did, the inside of a pawnbrokers. But they were happy, grateful, pleased with one another, and contented with the time. They ate their Christmas dinner of goose and pudding with great enjoyment and enthusiasm.

'At last the dinner was done, the cloth was cleared, the hearth swept, and the fire made up. The compound in the jug being tasted, and considered perfect, apples and oranges were put upon the table, and a shovel-full of chestnuts on the fire. Then all the Cratchit family drew round the hearth, in what Bob Cratchit called a circle, meaning half a one; and at Bob Cratchit's elbow stood the family display of glass. Two tumblers, and a custard-cup without a handle.

'These held the hot stuff from the jug, however, as well as golden goblets would have done; and Bob served it out with beaming looks, while the chestnuts on the fire sputtered and cracked noisily. Then Bob proposed:

"A Merry Christmas to us all, my dears. God bless us!" Which all the family re-echoed.'

Leader Let us spend a few moments in silence, thinking about our families, our parents and brothers and sisters.

—let us give thanks for them and all that they mean to us.
—let us recall the moments of joy we find in family life:
   sometimes, special occasions when the family are together,
   sometimes, very ordinary days when we hardly think about it,
   but we're just glad they're there.

Let us remember the times when we've disagreed with our families.

—the times when we've felt they didn't understand enough about us,
—or didn't seem to care enough about us,
—or they've worried too much about us,
—or the times when we've not thought enough about them.

Lord, we give thanks for our families:

that we can always turn to them and be at home,
that through our differences, we come to know each other and grow
together and know the joy of human love.

Amen.

Hymn   For the beauty of the earth.

(b) Discovering myself

Record   If I ruled the world (Harry Secombe.)

Leader   Today we shall listen to a selection of poems. They were all written by young people between the ages of 12–15 years. Each writer tries to express his own thoughts, feelings or dreams.

Voice   **Anger.**

Reader 1 Your whole mind filled to the brim
With hate, jealousy and anger.
It grows and grows until you swell
And overflows with the devil.
It burns an amber hole, black and poisoned
Through your soul,
Until anger, hate and jealousy win
By devouring your whole body up.
At last it rushes out full of poison
And deadly words.

Reader 2 Anger can well inside a person,
Then burst like a torrent of rain.
Anger can lose you your dearest friend
When you're in a stormy rage.
Some people when their tempers arise
Go out and viciously attack the nearest weed
To simmer down their raging tempers,
Or perhaps find solitude for a while
In a lonely room.

Voice   **Dreams.**

Reader 3 My burning desire is to help people.
To help anyone who is ill or lonely,

That is why I want to be a nurse.
So that I can help people when they are lonely,
To cheer up children who have something wrong with them.

I love looking after small children and babies,
Because of the time I first looked after my cousin.
I started dreaming how many children and adults
Needed love and care,
How some were crippled and had to be wheeled
Around in a chair,
How some are unable to see or hear
The things which are going on around them.

I myself would hate to be crippled or helpless,
That's why I want to be a nurse.
I wouldn't mind having a job in a welfare
Because I would still be able to help people;
To help them protect themselves from diseases.

Reader 4 As I walked through Birmingham town
Unnoticed by a soul
Amongst the hustle and bustle of the town
I was a single one.

But inside me I have a secret,
A good and wonderful ambition
I wish to be a craftsman
A craftsman of long ago.

Who would think of it,
Me, one ordinary person
To fight the battles of life alone.

Voice **Private Thoughts.**

Reader 5 There are some things in life
Which I would rather keep to myself.
I feel I would like to forget these
But something urges me to put them down on paper.
I sometimes feel very depressed and would like to cry.
I feel very hateful at times

13

And try to pull myself together
But it does no good.
Feelings of wanting to tell someone
Whirl through my mind.
The little feelings down beyond me,
I am afraid to tell anyone about them.
I am afraid they will laugh.

Leader   For our prayer we shall think about the words of a psalm which reminds us that God is always with us in all our thoughts and feelings.

Reader 6 O Lord, you search me and you know me,
You know my resting and my rising,
You discern my purpose from afar,
You mark when I walk or lie down,
All my ways lie open to you.

O where can I go from your spirit?
Or where can I flee from your face?
If I climb the heavens, you are there
If I lie in the grave, you are there

If I take the wings of the dawn
and dwell at the sea's furthest end,
Even there your hand would lead me,
and your right hand would hold me fast.

Your hand is ever upon me
You lead me and hold me fast.

(Psalm 139, Gelineau translation)

Record   If I ruled the world (*repeat*).
During this record the assembly disperses.

(c) School

Reader   Giving his report at the School Speech Day of Greenvalley Secondary School, the new headmaster of the school, Mr. J. P. Cooper, said that the first thing which had impressed him when he came to the school was the atmosphere he found there. Although he was doing his own individual work, each member of the school, he said, seemed to be aware that he had his own part to play in the school. He felt that people had a pride in the school and were working together to give it a fine community spirit. He then went on to describe some of the activities which had taken place during the school year which he said were excellent examples of this community spirit.

Voice A We come to school to learn skills which will equip us for life.

Voice B But we learn much more than reading and writing or how to cook or make a bookcase.

Voice C We also meet with people whose lives and ideas are very different from ours.

Voice A In all sorts of ways we learn how to live together and work together, and build a lively and interesting community.

Voice B A football or hockey team has to work together if the game is to be enjoyable or successful.

Voice C In the same way a choir has to be a team if it is to produce worthwhile singing.

Voice A The whole school works together, sometimes when it tries to raise money for a worthwhile cause.

Voice B There are all sorts of things going on in school which are extra to what we do in the classroom but which are all part of the school.
At this point, members of the school choir, football team, social service group, etc., could be asked to report briefly on some of these activities.

Leader All these things help to make our school into a community. The following reading might be called 'The Perfect Community'. It describes the life of the early Christians.

Reader Acts 2: 42–47.

Hymn Jesus, Lord, we look to thee.

Prayer Lord, we offer to you all our life here together.
We think of the friends we have made,

The new experiences we have shared,
And we give thanks for the richness this has brought to our lives.
As we bring to our school our own interests and talents,
Help us to work together, to share our gifts, and to work for the good of us all.

Amen.

(d) What is a friend?

Song Magic Penny.

Leader What is a friend? Today's readings try to explore this question. The first reading is from the most well known story of the Old Testament about friendship. King Saul ruled over Israel. His son Jonathan became such good friends with David that even though his father Saul threatened to kill David because he feared his success and popularity with the people, Jonathan did all he could to help David.

Reader 1 Samuel 19: 1–7.

Leader We shall now listen to a series of quotations from a book of cartoons. In the book, the central character Charlie Brown becomes depressed and feels that he has no friends. Other cartoon characters come along to try to cheer him up and they try to help him understand what a friend is. Combined with the cartoon drawings their definitions of 'a friend' make amusing reading, but they are also very thoughtful.

Voice A A friend is someone who's willing to watch the T.V. programme you want to watch.

Voice B A friend is someone who likes you even when the other boys are around.

Voice C A friend is someone who accepts you for what you are.

Voice D A friend is someone who is not jealous if you have other friends.

Voice E A friend is someone you have things in common with.

Voice A A friend is someone who likes the same music you like.

Voice B A friend is someone who can't stand the same sort of music you can't stand.

Voice C A friend is someone who will keep a place in the queue for you.

Voice D A friend is someone who sticks up for you when you're not there.

Voice E A friend is someone who doesn't criticize something you've just bought.

Leader For our prayers we shall say together two verses of a hymn by Charles Wesley.

Everybody

> Help us to help each other, Lord,
>   Each other's cross to bear,
> Let each his friendly aid afford,
>   And feel his brother's care.
>
> Help us to build each other up,
>   Our little stock improve,
> Increase our faith, confirm our hope,
>   And perfect us in love.
>   *Amen.*

(e) The length of friendship

Hymn The true light that enlightens man.

Leader Jesus said 'There is no greater love than this, that a man should lay down his life for his friends'. Our first two readings are true accounts of people who did precisely that.

Reader 1 Elizabeth Pilenko was a Polish nun interned at Ravensbrück concentration camp, as punishment for concealing Jewish fugitives from the hated Gestapo in a sanatorium she owned in France during the last world war. On Good Friday, 1945, just before the war in Europe came to an end, Elizabeth was watching the pathetic line of women being led to the gas chambers by the brutal guards. One young woman became hysterical, and Elizabeth succeeded in changing places with her when the guards were not watching.

Reader 2 Towards the end of 1964, in the Congo, a forty-five year old teacher from Dundee faced a terrible choice. Together with his friend William McChesney, an American Protestant missionary, he was arrested and condemned to death by the Congolese rebel army, not because he was a missionary, but because it was thought that he, like McChesney, came from the United States. McChesney had received rough treatment from his captors and was in poor health. James Rodger, the teacher, had been doing what he could for the American, and had only to prove his identity in order to be set free. He chose to say nothing and stay with his friend.

Leader Even if we are not challenged to the point of laying down our lives, a Japanese writer, however, suggests that to be a true friend calls for a great deal of hard work, thoughtfulness and service to others.

Reader 3 **The Good Neighbour.**
Bending neither to the rain
Nor to the wind
Nor to snow nor to summer heat,
Firm in body, yet
Without greed, without anger,
Always smiling serenely.
Eating his four cups of rough rice a day
With bean paste and a few vegetables,
Never taking himself into account
But seeing and hearing everything,
Understanding
And never forgetting.
If there is a sick child in the east
He goes and tends him.
If there is a tired mother in the west
He goes and shoulders her rice-sheaves.
Everyone calls him a fool.
Neither praised
Nor taken to heart.
That man
Is what I wish to be.

Prayers

18

Leader   There's nothing quite so enjoyable as a really
            good day out with our friends
                sharing our laughter
                enjoying our hobbies
                learning more about each other
                talking about our problems
            knowing that they will understand.

When our friends are around us
    we always know we have someone to talk to.
Help us to listen as well.

When our friends are around us
    we always know we have someone to help us.
Help us to recognize their needs as well.

When our friends are around us
    we always know we have someone to stand by us.
Help us to know what this means and to respond to it.

When our friends are around us,
    we always know that we are accepted.
Help us to give to others the trust they place in us.

                                    Amen.

Sources:
The poems on pages 10, 12–14 are from J. Beckett (ed.), *The Keen Edge*, Blackie and Son.
The quotations on Friendship on pages 16–17 are from Charles M. Schulz, 'I Need All The Friends I Can Get', Determined Productions, Inc.
Readers 1 and 2 on pages 17–18 are from Ian Birnie, *Encounter*, McGraw Hill Publishing Company.
The poem on page 18 is by Miyazawa Kenji and is from Geoffrey Bownas and Anthony Thwaite (translators), *Penguin Book of Japanese Verse*.

2 THE WORLD IN WHICH WE LIVE

(a) The world of work

Hymn   God of concrete, God of steel.

Leader   **The world in which we live.** A Hebrew poem describing the riches of the earth.

Voice A Surely there is a mine for silver, and a place for gold which they refine.

Voice B Iron is taken out of the earth, and copper is smelted from the ore.

Voice A Men put an end to darkness, and search out to the farthest bound the ore in gloom and deep darkness.

Voice B They open shafts in a valley away from where men live; they are forgotten by travellers, they hang afar from men, they swing to and fro.

Voice A As for the earth, out of it comes bread; but underneath it is turned up as by fire.

Voice B Its stones are the place of sapphires, and it has dust of gold.

Voice A Man cuts out channels in the rocks, and his eye sees every precious thing.

Voice B He binds up the streams so that they do not trickle, and the thing that is hid he brings forth to light.

(Job 28: 1–6, 10–11)

Leader   Man works with the materials of the earth.

Reader   The smith sits by the anvil, considering the unwrought iron. The vapour of the fire will waste his flesh; and in the heat of the furnace he will wrestle with his work. The noise of the hammer will be ever in his ears, and his eyes will be upon the pattern of the thing he is making. He will set his heart upon perfecting his work, and will be careful to polish it perfectly.

(Apocrypha)

Leader   By work each man makes his contribution to the world in which he lives.

Reader   All these trust in their hands, and each is skilful in his own work. Without them a town cannot be inhabited, and men cannot dwell there or go about their business. They shall not be sought for in the council of the people, nor sit in high places at the assembly. But they will maintain the fabric of the world, and in the handiwork of their craft is their prayer.

(Apocrypha)

Prayers   When we think about choosing a job, Lord, we think about all sorts of different things:

> is the pay good?
> what kind of holidays will we get?
> is the work interesting?
> what are the chances of promotion?

But we don't often think about why we work—apart from earning money to live.
Then we send for the doctor in the middle of the night,
Or we get up very early one morning and we meet a milkman on his rounds,
And see the morning train delivering the newspapers.

Lord, help us to value the work that every man does.
Help us to understand that when we do a job well
It is not just for our own satisfaction
But bit by bit we are building better towns and cities
And better lives for each other,
And we are giving something of ourselves to the world.

Song   Ballad of the Carpenter.

(b) Work: what do you get out of it?

Leader   Roy and Bob had not met since they left school, but now, seven years later, they have a good deal to talk about.

| Roy | Well, fancy you being married—and a dad as well! It makes me feel ancient, all my old mates married off. Time just flies, and you don't notice it going. I'll be on the shelf if I don't watch it. |

| Bob | You are so right. It doesn't seem two minutes since we were mad on basket ball, playing in the school team and licking all the other schools in the town. |

| Roy | Aye, a proper Harlem Globetrotters that team was! |

| Bob | You know, when I look back on school, the one thing I really enjoyed was the sport. I seem to remember you were good at most things; have you carried on since you left? |

| Roy | No, I couldn't be bothered; besides there's not much opportunity. |

| Bob | Oh, I don't know about that; most of the youth clubs have teams, and there's the athletics ground, not to mention works' teams. |

| Roy | Yes, but after a day in the factory I like to get out with the lads. You know, have a good time, only young once and all that! Still, now they are all getting hitched, I sometimes regret it. |

| Bob | How do you like your job? |

| Roy | Well I wouldn't use the word like. Let's say I go and come home again. It pays me a good wage, without working my backbone to a string of conkers that is. But I must say I hate the thought of sitting at that machine, turning out the same old bit of metal, day in day out, for the next fifty years. It's only by dreaming about how I'm going to spend the money, that keeps me from getting the twitches! |

| Bob | Not a pretty thought is it? Still there's hope for you yet, mate. How about coming down to the club I run, and helping me to coach the soccer team? Two nights a week, but I'll settle for one, how about it? |

| Roy | How much do they pay? |

| Bob | Pay, you must be joking. |

Roy   Not at all . . . you'd not catch me doing something for nothing, life's too short for that.

Leader   Compare the comments in that conversation with this description of an old watchmaker clearing up his workshop at the end of a day.

Reader   The watches put away, his eyes went to the clock that he was making in his spare moments. There had been no time to work at it tonight but he could spend a moment or two before it in adoration. He was always making a clock in his spare moments, most of them after the patterns of the older craftsmen whom he loved the best, but enriched always with some touch of genius that was all his own. For Isaac was artist as well as craftsman. He did not need to employ another man to design his clock cases or do his marquetry for him. What his imagination conceived his own brain and hand and eye could bring to perfection without help from another. He had no idea of money; he mostly forgot to send his bills in and he delighted in mending the watches of poor men for nothing. He had no idea either of the value of his clocks, but even if he had known that in the next century they would be eagerly sought after in the sale-rooms of Europe he would still have sold them as cheaply as he could to the men and women of the city because he loved the city. It was his city.

Hymn   Teach me, my God and King.

(c) Enjoying life

Leader   Today's readings are all on the theme of people enjoying themselves.

Reader 1 **The Song of a Sportsman.**
The Lord created man with a brain to help him enjoy life.
He gave man muscles and reflexes to kick, throw and catch a ball,
To dribble and shoot powerfully and accurately;
The eyes and anticipation to intercept a pass or a shot;
The agility and speed to catch a ball in the air;
The sense to play fairly and try not to injure fellow players;
To remain calm and unruffled when an incident occurs and not to retaliate;
To do what he is told and abide by the expert's decision;
To stay in a good humour whether he wins or loses
And to be thankful that he can play at all.

Reader 2 **Riding a Bicycle.**
Under the dawn I wake my two-wheel friend.
Shouting in bed my mother says to me,
'Mind you don't clatter it going downstairs!'
I walk him down he springing step to step:
those tyres he has, if you pat him flat-handed
he'll bounce your hand. I mount with an air
and as light a pair of legs as you'll encounter,
slow into Sunday ride out of the gates,
roll along asphalt, press down on the pedals,
speeding, fearless, ring, ring, ring.

Flinging along my happiness my fever,
incapable of breaking out of it,
overtaking the lorries on the road
taking each of them in a single swoop
flying behind them through cut open space
hanging on them uphill. Yes I know.
It's dangerous. I enjoy it. They hoot
and lean out and yell out,
'We'll give you a hand on the hills;
give you some speed; after that
you tear along on your own.'
Careering full tilt, pelting along
in a flurry of jokes. Turn a blind eye
to my crazy career; it's the fashion.
You can't tell me how terribly I ride.
One day I'll learn how to ride.
And I spring down at a deserted
ancient lodge by the roadside,
in dim forest light I break lilac,
twine it with ivy on to the handlebars.
Flying on, flying,
sticking my face down into dark blossom,
get into the city quite worn out.

Leader   Let us pray.
Thank you, O God, for the five main gifts that you have given us:
    the eyes that you have given us to see the beautiful things in the
       world; for instance, the flowers that go forward in the breeze,

the sense of smell with which we can smell delicious foods and the salty smell of the sea which is very savoury indeed,

the virtue of conversation by which we can speak to other people, and we learn something by talking things over and it might change our whole way of life,

the gift of hearing by which we can hear the sweet and dramatic music, and all the everyday noises like the milkman when he comes clattering down the street on his morning round, the rent man, the baker, and many other men,

the most wonderful virtue of all—the mind which tells all our other senses what to do.

Song   Thank you.

(d) Everybody needs help

Record   Help (Beatles).

Voice A   When you think of all the problems in the world, people starving, diseased, illiterate, we are really very well off, aren't we? I mean although people in this country don't exactly live a life of luxury, most people have a roof over their heads, enough food and clothes, and everyone has a reasonable education, don't they?

Voice B   Yes, that's true, but quite a lot of people need help in other ways.

Voice A   What do you mean?

Voice B   Well, people have hidden needs—things you might not notice if you didn't really bother to look or you didn't think about it.

Leader   Volunteers who have helped with all kinds of problems speak:

Reader 1 **Hospitals:** '. . . The great frustration is that so much more could be done for the children if only there were more staff, more money, more time, more interest. The nurses on the ward simply did not have the time or the inclination to play with or amuse the children, and these children thrive on affection. I hate to think of the "runabouts" having no one particularly to take notice of them.'

Reader 2 **New Towns:** '. . . K. hasn't the problems which are to be found in the older established towns. However, the fact that there are no slums should not be a matter to lament! The problems are different, difficult and new— so present a new hard challenge. The townspeople do not know their town and sometimes do not care to know it. K. does not provide interesting amenities. The pensioners have been separated from their families. Many of the youngsters are unused to any responsibility and are consequently hard to keep in touch with. But don't let this put anyone off. They are wonderful people to work with and those who do volunteer, often the scruffiest, have produced some fine results. The few who do show enthusiasm are enough to make up for the many who don't, and *they* still remain the challenge, those who could be encouraged to do something.'

Reader 3 **Handicapped Children:** '. . . the youngest were five (years). They needed someone to make a fuss of them at times. But as well as needing to be cared for they also needed to care for someone else themselves. The older ones would enjoy helping me to dress the younger and slower ones for play. They would help me over stiles when we were out for a walk, and a great privilege was being allowed to clean my shoes. . . . One thing that all the boys, especially the very handicapped ones, showed me was courage. I came to admire and respect them very greatly for it. A boy with very little co-ordination would struggle for half an hour, if one let him, to do up his shirt button. They were never willing to give in and I think could show the unhandicapped person a good deal.'

Hymn Where cross the crowded ways of life (preferably sung to the tune Crantock by M. Brierley from *Thirty 20th Century Hymn Tunes*).

Prayer Lord, it is difficult for us to understand the unhappiness in the world,
To realize that people suffer and need help in all sorts of ways,
And even sometimes most difficult to think how we might help.
We're so busy with our own lives
                    our own happiness
                    our own cares
                    our own problems
that we can't always see the unhappiness, the fears, the problems of others,
and we can't always find the time to help.

But we want to live in a better world, Lord;
A world where people work together rather than fight

where suspicion is broken down by friendliness
where selfishness is replaced by service.
Help us to realize that everybody needs help, everybody in the world.
May we never be too proud to ask for help nor so selfish
    that we fail to offer our help to others.

Amen.

(e) Losing yourself

Hymn   Fill Thou my life, O Lord my God.

Leader   It has been said that one of the features of this modern generation is that it is not prepared to keep silent in face of what it believes to be wrong. Perhaps this is why demonstrations and protests are now almost a regular part of news bulletins. It is worth remembering that young people demonstrate their concern not only by placards and marches, but also in more positive and less dramatic ways. Many school groups have organized sponsored walks for Oxfam or Shelter, and thousands of young people regularly give up some of their spare time to visiting the old or handicapped in their area.

Mention here any similar schemes which may operate in your school and where possible ask one or more of the pupils involved to report on their activities and describe their experiences.

The first reading is from a newspaper article, written in 1966, describing a boy who volunteered to work for a month in a Cheshire Home.

Reader   'Dennis Tucker is a Rocker whose thick curly hair folds down over the collar of his studded leather jacket, whose 650 c.c. Triumph proclaims all the badges of the "roar around a town" brigade. Dennis had done it all: ridden in packs to the South Coast and notched his share of tons and mixed it with Mods—"you know, burned 'em off and all".
But Dennis is another kind of tough guy.
While his lot were revving outside the pubs and caffs of Yorkshire's North Riding, he caught a train to London and joined the Community Service Volunteers.
Within twenty-four hours he was assigned to St. Cecilia's Cheshire Home in Bromley, Kent, to care for people stricken with diseases that make them almost incapable of doing anything for themselves. His patience with the stricken is positively therapeutic. He lights their cigarettes, reads to them,

washes and shaves them. "It's amazing how they respond", he said. "With coaxing, one chap has begun to dress himself."

The elixir is his youth. It's infectious. Mr. David Floom has been seven years in St. Cecilia's. He said, "The sound of a dropped tray followed by a boy's laughter does more good to ease my lot than rubber-tyred wheels on lino floors."

"I don't know why", he said. "Birds and bikes and work aren't everything. I just wanted to do something that really counts." '

Leader The second reading describes the thoughts of another volunteer.

Reader 'The first point I want to make about what it means to be a Community Service Volunteer: it means being away from home and it means being away for long periods.

The second point is that it means you are left alone to work out your own salvation. In other words you have to use your own initiative. Being a volunteer means being on your own. It means that your problems have to be solved by you—there is rarely a chance to take them to a higher authority. Being on your own also means that you have only yourself to answer to. You may work for an institution or body—in fact you certainly will—but they will rarely pass an opinion on what they think of you. You, however, will know exactly how successful you have been because only you will be able to assess your own work.

Being a volunteer does not mean a steady job. There are occasions when you wish it were. It would be lovely to be able to put a limit on your work and say, "Well, it's five o'clock now so I can't do that—it will have to wait until morning"—because being a volunteer means that the job takes as long as it lasts. One thing you realize from the very beginning is that, unlike an ordinary job, the amount of work expected of you is not proportional to the pay.

Finally, being a volunteer means finding, or if necessary first losing, yourself. You don't change the world: you probably don't achieve anything material at all, but you do emerge at the other end of your spell of voluntary work not necessarily a better person, but a person who knows himself much better, and this is surely the ultimate meaning of being a volunteer.'

Reading 1 John 3: 16–19.

Prayer Lord, you have taught us that
    whoever seeks to save his life will lose it,

and whoever loses it will save it,
and live.
For all the times when we have seen
the needs of others and responded
and found satisfaction and happiness
in working for other people,
we give thanks.
Help us to understand that in serving others
we are serving you,
discovering ourselves,
and discovering a little more
of the meaning of true life.
Amen.

Sources:
The dialogue on pages 21–23 is from Ian Birnie, *Encounter*, McGraw Hill Publishing Company.
The reading on page 23 is from Elizabeth Goudge, *The Dean's Watch*, Hodder and Stoughton.
'The Song of a Sportsman' on page 23 and the prayer on pages 24–25 are from R. Hearn (compiler) *Modern Psalms by Boys*, University of London Press.
'Riding a Bicycle' on page 24 is by Yevtushenko and is from Peter Levi and Robin Milner Gulland (translators), *Selected Poems*, Penguin.
Readers 1, 2 and 3 on pages 25–26 and the reading on page 28 are reprinted with permission from the annual report of Community Service Volunteers.
The reading on pages 27–28 is from *The Daily Mirror*.

3 THE WIDER WORLD

(a) All the lonely people

Record   Eleanor Rigby (Beatles).

Reader 1 **The Face of Loneliness.**

Name: Annie Gosling.

Age: 92.

Address: Cecil Road, Exeter.

Problem: Loneliness.
'I've been alone in the world since my dear husband died six months ago.
You can't expect people to come and see you very often, but it would be
nice if they did.
There are times I feel sad, so very sad, and unwanted. I feel useless because
no one needs me.
If I could put my hat on and go out it wouldn't be so bad—but I'm too
sick and tired to walk alone.
I wish I had someone to talk to and be with all the time. It's no use being
old these days, you're just a burden.'

Reader 2 **The Face of Loneliness.**
'Dear Daddy.' In her best handwriting eleven year old Jane wrote a letter
to her make-believe father every week. She addressed the envelope to
herself, and every week without fail she wrote back—'Dear Jane'. For this
shy youngster living in a local authority home two 4d. stamps and a dream
father were the only cure she had available for an affliction that is so
pathetically easy to diagnose—LONELINESS. At this moment there are
four million desperately lonely people in this country. Before someone like
young Jane grows into a lonely Mrs. X. I know who rings up the telephone
speaking clock for company, why don't we ACT?'

Reader 3 **The Face of Loneliness.**

'. . . and so, we bid you a very pleasant good night!' Often she used to turn on the radio in the evening, just as the programme ended, in order to hear those few words, in order to hear a human voice wish her goodnight. Yet, she worked as a secretary of an international welfare organization. Her boss, a fine man, had dedicated his whole life to the battle against a social scourge. Many visitors from every country came to see him, but in the office they spoke only business. Never was there a word addressed to her as a person. Who she was, how she, a foreigner, had come to Geneva after many ups and downs, the sorrows that still deeply troubled her—nobody cared about these things. Her work was appreciated, and she received every courtesy, but to all intents and purposes she remained alone.

She lived in one of those great modern buildings, with countless one-room flats, where the neighbours' noises come from every floor. She knew none of those neighbours with whom she rubbed shoulders in the elevator daily, and they did not know her. She had no intimate friends. Her room was even in the same building where she worked. She rarely went out for any reason except for the odd hurried shopping trip. Before falling asleep, she would switch on the radio, '. . . and so, we bid you a very pleasant good night!' It was a human voice, speaking *to her*.

Leader Let us pray.

There are two loves only, Lord, love of myself and love of you and of others,
And each time that I love myself, it's a little less love for you and for others.
What is more serious, Lord, is that love of self is a stolen love.
It was destined for others, they needed it to live, to thrive, and I have
    diverted it.
So the love of self creates human suffering,
So the love of men for themselves creates human misery,
All the miseries of men,
All the sufferings of men:

> The suffering of the boy whose mother has slapped him without cause,
>   and that of the man whose boss has reprimanded him in front of the
>   other workers;
> The suffering of the ugly girl neglected at a dance, and that of the
>   woman whose husband doesn't kiss her any more;
> The suffering of the child left at home because he's a nuisance, and
>   that of the grandfather made fun of because he's too old;

All sufferings are an unappeased hunger, a hunger for love.

Grant me Lord to spread true love in the world.

31

Grant that it may penetrate into offices, factories, apartment buildings, cinemas, dance halls.

Help me to love Lord, not to waste my powers of love; to love myself **less** and less in order to love others more and more,

That around me, no one should suffer or die because I have stolen the love they needed to live.

Song   Can I see another's woe.

(b) Modern Samaritans

Reader 1 Luke 10: 29–37.

Reader 2 Old Mrs. Jackson lived alone in a small flat in London. She seldom had visitors and because of her age and poor health, she was not able to go out very much. When she became ill, it was three days before anyone realized it. Her next door neighbour said, 'I did notice that I hadn't seen or heard her, but my little boy had measles and I was too busy to pop in to see her.' The milkman said, 'I thought it was a bit funny that she hadn't picked up her milk, but I was late yesterday and couldn't stop to see if she was all right.'

The man in the Post Office on the corner said, 'I must say, she usually comes in for her pension on Tuesday, but when she didn't come I thought she'd decided to come on Wednesday instead. It never really occurred to me she might be ill.'

Leader   Unfortunately, stories such as this one are not unknown and if we read our newspapers, particularly looking for stories of people in need, we should find quite a number. It is not difficult in these days to discover stories of people who are ill or lonely and in despair. Sometimes, people find the problems of life completely overwhelming and so great is their helplessness and despair that they even think of taking their own life.

Today we shall listen to an account of an organization started by a man who was anxious to try to help those, who, because of the problems they had met in their lives, had come to this extreme point of despair.

Reader 3 **The Samaritans.**

Chad Varah, an Anglican priest, became Rector of St. Stephen Walbrook in the City of London in 1953. The week before he moved there from

Battersea, he buried a girl of 18 who had killed herself; or, as we said in those days when it was a crime, 'committed suicide.' The coroner at her inquest suggested that she might not have killed herself if someone had been there to listen to her troubles. Chad Varah determined to use his city church and a telephone to listen to suicidal people. He put a small-ad in a London evening newspaper and received twenty-seven calls in the first week.

Soon he was listening, and counselling twelve hours a day. He asked some of his congregation to make cups of tea for the people waiting in the outer vestry; and he found that some of his clients, including some in the deepest distress, were different people by the time they got to him. Indeed some of them went away without even seeing him, for they had already been 'befriended' by the helpers in the outer vestry. He decided to train the lay helpers to answer the telephone calls for help, and to befriend clients away from the church as well as on the premises. So the Samaritans were born; and now nearly all the telephone-answering and all the befriending is done by laymen.

In 1959 another post was opened in Edinburgh. Churches or groups of laymen—interdenominational from the start, even in Ireland—started posts in Belfast, Glasgow, Liverpool, Manchester, Birmingham and other cities. Now there are ninety-two posts operating in the United Kingdom, and in fact there are only a few gaps to be filled to complete national coverage.

Voice A How big is the problem?

Voice B Over 6,000 persons a year commit suicide in the United Kingdom. The number of unsuccessful attempts is probably ten times as great as the number of those who actually commit suicide.

Voice A This means that a very large number of people find themselves in situations of extreme distress and despair. What is the cause of their despair?

Voice B Apart from loneliness—both in those who are socially isolated and in those whose relatives lack understanding and whose friends 'don't want to know'—the despair which leads to suicide may arise from such things as mental illness, emotional disturbances, spiritual difficulties, addiction to drugs, alcohol or gambling, lack of accommodation or employment, debt, crime; physical illness or infirmity. It is estimated that about 45 per cent of those who do commit suicide had psychiatric problems and about 55 per cent required either non-medical counselling or the support of loving friends and relations, or both.

Voice A What happens when a person who doubts whether he can bear to go on living because 'nobody cares' telephones a Branch of the Samaritans?

Voice B In most cases he finds that the person at the other end is not an 'expert' who knows all the answers but a compassionate fellow human being who may not know any of the answers but who makes it impossible to say that 'nobody cares', and who is comfortably aware that there are people within the organization who know most of the answers. Sooner or later, usually sooner, the sad story is elicited and a competent person decides what is to be done about it and by whom. Whatever other arrangements are made, in nearly every case 'befriending' will be prescribed, sometimes by more than one of the Samaritans and sometimes very intensively. It has been found in practice that even in very serious situations, befriending by an experienced Samaritan may be the only thing necessary, though a considerable proportion of clients also receive counselling or treatment and a few do not require befriending at all.
The Samaritans aim not only to keep people alive but to help them to be glad to be alive.

Record There but for fortune (Joan Baez).

Leader Let us keep silence for a few moments.
Pause.
Today, Lord,
we think about those who are not glad to be alive,
        those who are mentally ill,
                or emotionally disturbed,
        those who are addicted to drugs, alcohol or gambling,
                the unemployed, the homeless,
                the infirm and the lonely;
All those for whom life has become a burden rather than a joy.
Help us to meet those who are in need
                with compassion and understanding,
        to support those who are working
                to relieve human suffering,
        and grant us to spread true love in the world.
                                    Amen.

34

(c) A roof over your head

Reader 1 An advertisement: Furnished flat to let in purpose-built block. Lift, constant hot water, housekeeper. Central heating, Reception Room, Two Bedrooms, Dining Hall, Kitchen, Bathroom. Beautifully decorated and furnished throughout. Twenty guineas per week.

Reader 2 Mr. & Mrs. W. and their four children paid £4 15s. 0d. a week for two rooms in Birmingham. One room was so damp that it was totally unusable in the winter and the family lived in the kitchen. Mrs. W. slept most nights sitting upright in an armchair with a child on each arm. She said that when they did sleep in the larger room she often found their baby like a drowned rat in the mornings. Twenty-seven people shared the one toilet and one cold water tap. The house was in an appalling condition and there was a family in every room . . .

Song 'It's a funny old world.' (Preferably this song should be sung, although if this is not possible it may be read.)

or

'Shelter.'

Leader The Government White Paper of 1965 on Housing stated, 'In Great Britain some three million families still live in slums, near slums or grossly overcrowded conditions.'

Reader 1 *London*: In London, over 150,000 families are on Council waiting lists. Half a million people are over-crowded; 7,000 are in hostels for the homeless; more than 50,000 of its houses are unfit for human habitation.

Reader 2 *Glasgow*: 80,000 families in Glasgow are on the local authority waiting list. 100,000 (one third) of its houses are unfit, one third of its population is overcrowded.

Reader 1 *Birmingham*: Nearly 40,000 families in Birmingham are on Council waiting lists. Over 40,000 houses are unfit and more than 115,000 people are living in overcrowded conditions; more than 250 families are in hostels for the homeless.

Leader Suppose a brother or a sister is in rags and one of you says, 'Good luck to you, keep warm', but does nothing to supply their bodily needs, what is the good of that? (James 2: 15–16.)

Reader 2 Lord, I can't sleep; I have got up out of bed to pray,
And the lights of the city, signs of the living, pierce the darkness.
I cannot escape them, Lord; I know their sufferings too well.
I see them rising before me,
I hear them speaking to me,
I feel them hitting me.

I know that in one single room thirteen crowded people are
breathing on one another.
I know that rats come out to eat the crusts and bite the babies.
I know a father who gets up to stretch oil-cloth above the rain-soaked
bed of his four children.
I know a mother who stays up all night since there is room for only
one bed, and the two children are sick.
I know a drunken father who vomits on the child sleeping beside him.
I know a big boy who runs away alone into the night because he
can't stand it any more.
I know hundreds of others—yet I was going to sleep peacefully
between my clean white sheets.

I wish I didn't know, Lord,
I wish it were not true,
I wish I could convince myself that I'm dreaming,
I've seen too much,
I've counted too much, and, Lord, these ruthless figures have robbed
me for ever of my innocent peace.

Reader 3 So much the better, son;
For I, your God, your Father, am angry with you.
I gave you the world at the beginning of time, and I want each of my sons
to have a home worthy of their Father, in my vast kingdom.
I trusted you, and your selfishness has spoiled everything.

Come, son, ask forgiveness for yourself and for others tonight.
And, tomorrow, fight with all your strength, for it hurts your Father to see
that once more there is no room for his son at the inn.

Hymn O brother man, fold to thy heart thy brother.

Prayer Lord, we sit in the comfort of our own homes,
Where we have space, and warmth, and peace.
And often we don't want to know about the problems of others.

We put down the newspaper and we turn off the television
When we see uncomfortable facts which we'd rather not know.
Forgive us for our lack of care and help us to understand the real problems
of those who have no proper home of their own.

Help us to turn our understanding into action so that we shall continually
look for ways we can help bring about your kingdom on earth.
Help us to use our time, our minds, our energies, our money, through work
and political action,
To help those in this country and overseas who are without homes and
almost without hope.

Amen.

(d) Black and white don't mix

Leader The Institute of Race Relations has estimated that by 1965 a total of
820,000 coloured people were living in Britain. By far the largest group is
from the West Indies, with an approximate total of 430,000. The Indians
number approximately 165,000, Pakistanis 100,000, and those from other
countries in Africa and Asia, 125,000.
The main reason why immigrants have come to Britain is that they were
looking for better opportunities for themselves and their families. Coming
from poor, underdeveloped countries, they hope to find better housing,
better work, and better education than they could expect to find at home.
Do they find it?

Reader 1 Mr. Ken Shepherd is a Jamaican who has been living in England since
1955. He is employed as a higher-grade postman; his wife, who was also
born in Jamaica, is a district nurse and midwife. They are both dark-
skinned. Their three children are Londoners by birth.
Mrs. Shepherd has a car, which she uses every day for her work. In the
Tooting area of South London, where they lived, she had nowhere to
garage it, and used to park it in the street at night. It suffered damage from
hooligans, and was often hard to start on cold mornings.
The Shepherds, who had been saving for a long time to buy their own
home, decided that when the time came to choose a house, they would
look for one with a garage. This decision eventually led them, in September
1967, to a quiet residential street in South Norwood, where there was a
semi-detached house, complete with garage, for sale.
After having the property examined by a surveyor, the Shepherds agreed

to buy it for £5,800. Mr. Shepherd obtained from a building society the offer of a mortgage of £3,800, repayable over a period of 25 years, and on the strength of this paid a first deposit of £100 to the estate agent.

The Shepherds were anxious to complete the transaction and move into their new home as soon as possible.

Then, on 27th September, they discovered that the deal had fallen through. Their prospective neighbours in the street had formed a property syndicate to buy the house and thus prevent its occupation by a coloured family. Through private negotiation, by-passing the agent, the vendor had accepted the neighbour's offer of £5,700, and a contract was being prepared for immediate signature.

One of the new purchasers was reported by *The Daily Mirror* to have said, 'We are not racialists. Our motives are mercenary. I believe that if a coloured family had arrived next door, our houses would have been devalued by between £1,000 and £1,500.'

Residents of the street were interviewed by David Frost in a television programme. Some dissociated themselves from the action taken by the neighbours' syndicate. One man said firmly that he *did* want to 'keep the street white', and when asked for his reasons replied, 'They cause trouble, and keep all-night parties.' As if to clinch the argument, he added, 'Black and white don't mix.'

Leader Political and Economic Planning (P.E.P. for short), an organization which made a detailed study of the subject and published its findings in April 1967, says its investigation revealed substantial discrimination against coloured immigrants in employment, housing and the provision of services. It concluded, 'There is little doubt that the discrimination is largely based on colour.'

Reader 2 This is an extract from a letter written by the late Dr. Martin Luther King, the Civil Rights Leader in the United States. It speaks of the American situation, which is a little different from that of Britain, but more importantly it describes what it feels like to be treated as an inferior—simply because your skin is black.

'You seek to explain to your six-year-old daughter why she can't go to the public amusement park that has just been advertised on television, and see tears welling up when she is told that Funtown is closed to coloured children, and see the depressing clouds of inferiority begin to form in her little mental sky, and see her begin to distort her personality by unconsciously developing a bitterness toward white people. You have to concoct an answer for a five-year-old son asking, "Daddy, why do white people treat coloured people so mean?" You take a cross-country drive and find it necessary to sleep night after night in the uncomfortable corners of your automobile because no motel will accept you. You are humiliated day in and day out by nagging signs reading "white" men and "coloured". Your first name becomes "nigger" and your middle name becomes "boy" (however old you are) and your last name becomes "John", and your wife and mother are never given the respected title "Mrs".'

Reader 3 It is a Christian duty to treat every human being as a creation of God himself, as a brother for whom Christ died, as one who is as Christ himself to us. 'Inasmuch as ye have done it unto one of the least of these my brethren, ye have done it unto me.' I challenge any Christian man to state that it is conceivable that any restriction of colour or race was in Christ's mind when he uttered these words. And the words are the death of 'problems'. No man, no set of men, may be a problem to a Christian man—a race problem, a colour problem, an economic problem. 'Am I my brother's keeper?' The inescapable answer is—you are.

Hymn In Christ there is no east or west.

Leader The following is from one of the most famous speeches of Dr. Martin Luther King when at a rally he addressed a very large number of people from the steps of the Lincoln Memorial in Washington.

Record The Martin Luther King speech beginning, 'I have a Dream.'

(If it is not possible to use this record, a reader could read the following extract from it.)

'I have a dream that one day this nation will rise up and live out the true meaning of its creed: "We hold these truths to be self evident: that all men are created equal." I have a dream that one day on the red hills of Georgia, the sons of former slaves and the sons of former slave owners, will be able to sit down together at the table of brotherhood. I have a dream that one day even the state of Mississippi, a state sweltering with the heat of injustice, sweltering with the heat of oppression, will be transformed into an oasis of freedom and justice. I have a dream that my four little children will one day live in a nation where they will not be judged by the colour of their skin, but by the content of their character. I have a dream today.'

Prayer   Lord, we pride ourselves on being fair,
        on giving every man an equal chance.
      Help us to understand ourselves.
      We are often suspicious and even afraid
        of those whose language is different from ours,
        of those whose customs are different from ours,
        of those whose colour is different from ours.
      Help us to understand our fears, to break down the barriers of suspicion
        and mistrust which we build against those who are different.
      Help us to see that we are all members of your world.
      Fill us with your love so that we may live together and work
        together as neighbours and brothers in your world.

                                                          Amen.

(e) This hungry world

Reading   Luke 9: 14–17.

Song   Feed us now.

Leader   The first reading is a description written by a man who had lived for a few years in a poor region of Jamaica.

Reader 1 'Often I woke in the morning to the sound of the Barrett family scratching away with their "machettes" (a kind of cutlass) at the surface soil of a small field they rented next to my house. All the children over the age of four helped to cultivate the soil and weed the crops.

Mr. Barrett's smallholding (total extent, less than two acres) wasn't big enough to support the family. The soil was poor, the rainfall uncertain. Sometimes a complete crop failed mysteriously. At the best of times the family existed on a poorly-balanced diet. At the worst of times, the children were hungry.

While I was living there, one of the children, aged about 12 months, became ill and died. The death certificate recorded the cause of death as "Malnutrition". I conducted the child's burial service in the backyard of the Barrett home.

It wasn't the first time Mrs. Barrett had suffered the loss of a child. Altogether she had had twelve children, of whom eight had survived. When I knew the family, she was between 36 and 37 years old, and capable of having several more children. How the Barrett home could accommodate any more was far from clear. It consisted of three small rooms—a living room and two bedrooms.

Whether Mr. Barrett could support any more children was also questionable. It was almost impossible for him to supplement his income from his smallholding by doing casual work; the area where he lived was one of high unemployment, and unskilled work was hard to come by.

Mr. and Mrs. Barrett, although poor, were by no means the poorest people in the neighbourhood and serve to illustrate problems which are real and pressing all over Jamaica, and throughout the Caribbean, Latin America, Africa and Asia.'

Leader   The world we live in.

Reader 2   In 1963, 125 million babies were born. This works out at 238 per minute or four every second.

Reader 3   Between 1925 and 1962, the population of Latin America doubled to its present figure of 218 millions. But the production of food in Latin America has not increased since 1939.

Reader 2   In most countries of Latin America, Africa and Asia, between 40 and 45 per cent of the population is under the age of 15. Within a few years' time, they will themselves be bearing children.

Reader 3   In 1867, there were only five cities in the world with more than one million inhabitants. In 1967 there were 120 cities in the world with more than a million inhabitants.

Reading   Matthew 25: 34–40.

Prayers   I have eaten,
I have eaten too much,
I have eaten only because others have done so,
Because I was invited,
Because I was in the world and the world would not have understood;
And each dish
And each mouthful
And each morsel was hard to get down.
I have eaten too much, Lord,
While at that moment, in my town, more than 1,500 persons queued up
at the bread line,

41

While in her attic a woman ate what she had salvaged that morning
                                        from the garbage bins,
While urchins in their orphanage divided some scraps from the old
                                        folks' home.
While ten, a hundred, a thousand unfortunates throughout the
    world, at that very moment twisted in pain and died of hunger
                                        before their despairing families.
Lord, it's terrible, for I know,
Men know, now.
They know that not only a few destitute are hungry, but hundreds at
                                        their own doors.
They know that not only several hundreds but thousands are hungry
                                        on the borders of their country,
They know that not only thousands, but millions, are hungry
                                        throughout the world.
'. . . I was hungry . . .'
It's you who queue up at the bread line,
It's you who eat the scraps of garbage,
It's you who are tortured by hunger and starve to death,
It's you who die alone in a corner at 26,
While in another corner of the great hall of the world, with some members
    of our family, I eat without being hungry, what is needed to save you.

'. . . I was hungry . . .'
Remind me of that, Lord, if I cease for a moment to give myself.
I'll never be through giving bread to my brothers, for there are too
                                        many of them.
There'll always be some who won't have had their share.
I'll never be through fighting to get bread for all my brothers.

Hymn   When I needed a neighbour.

Sources:
Readings 1, 2 and 3 on pages 30–31 are from *The Daily Mirror*, *The Daily Express* and Paul Tournier, *Escape From Loneliness*, S.C.M. Press, respectively.
The prayer on pages 31–32, Readers 2 and 3 on page 36 and the prayer on pages 41–42 are from Michel Quoist, *Prayers of Life*, Gill and Macmillan.
The material on pages 32–34 is from Samaritan Leaflets.
Reader 1 on pages 37–38 and Reader 1 on pages 40–41 are from *Probe*, C.E.M.
Reader 3 on page 39 is from *Racialism in South Africa*, published by South African Church Institute.

4 TIMES AND SEASONS

(a) The beginning of term

Hymn   O Praise ye the Lord.

Voice A   For everything there is a season,
and a time for every matter under heaven:

Voice B   a time to be born, and a time to die;

Voice A   a time to plant, and a time to pluck up what is planted;

Voice B   a time to weep, and a time to laugh;

Voice A   a time to seek, and a time to lose;

Voice B   a time to keep, and a time to cast away;

Voice A   a time to rend, and a time to sew;

Voice B   a time to love, and a time to hate;

Voices   For everything there is a season,
A & B   and a time for every matter under heaven.   (Eccles. 3: 2-8)

Leader   As we return from our holidays, when we've had an opportunity for a
change and a rest, once again we begin to fill our lives with all the things
which so regularly take up our time. We shall begin this term by thinking
about time and how we spend it.

Voice A   I went out, Lord.
Men were coming out.
They were coming and going,
Walking and running.
Everything was rushing, cars, lorries, the street, the whole town.

43

Men were rushing not to waste time.
They were rushing after time,
To catch up with time,
To gain time.

Voice B Goodbye, sir, excuse me, I haven't time.

Voice C I'll come back, I can't wait, I haven't time.

Voice D I must end this letter, I haven't time.

Voice E I'd love to help you, but I haven't time.

Voice F I can't accept, having no time.

Voice B I can't think, I can't read, I'm swamped, I haven't time.

Voice C I'd like to pray, but I haven't time.

Voice A You understand, Lord, they simply haven't the time.

Voice D The child is playing, he hasn't time right now . . . Later on . . .

Voice E The schoolboy has his homework to do, he hasn't time . . . Later on . . .

Voice F The student has his courses, and so much work, he hasn't time . . . Later on . . .

Voice B The young man is at his sports, he hasn't time . . . Later on . . .

Voice C The young married man has his new house, he has to fix it up, he hasn't time . . . Later on . . .

Voice D The grandparents have their grandchildren, they haven't time . . . Later on . . .

Voice E They are ill, they have their treatments, they haven't time . . . Later on . . .

Voice F They are dying, they have no . . .

Voice B Too late! . . . They have no more time!

Voice A And so all men run after time, Lord.
They pass through life running—hurried, jostled, overburdened,
                              frantic, and they never get there. They haven't time.
In spite of all their efforts they're still short of time,
                              of a great deal of time.
Lord, you must have made a mistake in your calculations.
There is a big mistake somewhere.
The hours are too short,
The days are too short,
Our lives are too short.

Leader Let us pray.

For all the variety we find in life
     for times and seasons
     for work and recreation.

Response We give thanks.

Leader For the memory of holidays
     new places visited
     new friendships made
     new experiences gained.

Response We give thanks.

Leader For the time that you give us
     time to work and to rest
     time for ourselves
     and time for others

Response We give thanks.

Leader Let us think in silence of the holiday we have just had and think ahead to the term which is just starting. Let us give thanks that there are times when we can be quiet, when we can look at our lives and come to know ourselves and our friends a little better, and we can begin to understand a little more of the world in which we live.
Pause.

Leader Let us say the grace together.

45

All   May the grace of our Lord Jesus Christ
  and the love of God
  and the fellowship of the Holy Spirit
  be with us now and always.
                    Amen.

Record   If I only had time (John Rowles).

(b) The end of term

Hymn   All creatures of our God and King.

Voice A   In the beginning
  God created the heaven and the earth
  And he made darkness and light.

Voice B   He divided the waters from the dry land
  And the dry land brought forth grass and trees
  And the living creatures dwelt in the sea and on the earth.

Voice C   And God created man in his own image, male and female.

Voice D   And God saw everything that he had made and behold it was very good.

Voice E   And God rested from his work.

Reader   **A Day at the Seaside.**
  In a huddle of picnicking women and their children, stretched out limp
  and damp in the sweltering sun or fussing over paper carriers or building
  castles that were at once destroyed by the tattered march of other pic-
  nickers to different pieces of the beach, among the ice-cream cries, the
  angrily happy shouts of boys playing ball, and the screams of girls as the
  sea rose to their waists, the young man sat alone. Some silent husbands,
  with rolled up trousers and suspenders dangling, paddled slowly on the
  border of the sea, paddling women, in thick, black picnic dresses, laughed
  at their own ankles, dogs chased stones, and one proud boy rode the water
  on a rubber seal. The young man, in his wilderness, saw the holiday
  Saturday set down before him, false and pretty, the disporting families
  with paper bags, buckets and spades, parasols and bottles, the happy, hot,
  and aching girls with sunburn liniments in their bags, the bronzed young

46

men with chests, and the envious, white young men in waistcoats, the thin, pale, pathetic legs of the husbands silently walking through the water, the plump and curly, shaven-headed and bowed-backed children up to no sense with unrepeatable delight in the dirty sand, moved him. He caught the ball that a small boy had whacked into the air with a tin tray, and rose to throw it back.

The boy invited him to play. A friendly family stood waiting some way off, the tousled women with their dresses tucked up, the bare-footed men in shirt sleeves, a number of children in slips and cut-down underwear. He bowled to a father standing with a tray before the wicket of hats. The tray whirled and he chased the ball towards the sea, passing undressing women with a rush and a wink, tripping over a castle into a coil of wet girls lying like snakes, soaking his shoes as he grabbed the ball off a wave, he felt his happiness return in a boast of the body, and, 'Look out, Duckworth, here's a fast one coming,' he cried to the mother behind the hats. The ball bounced on a boy's head. In and out of the scattered families, among the sandwiches and clothes, uncles and mothers fielded the bouncing ball. A bald man, with his shirt hanging out returned it in the wrong direction, and a collie carried it into the sea. Now it was mother's turn with the tray. Tray and ball together flew over her head. An uncle in a panama smacked the ball to the dog, who swam with it out of reach. They offered the young man egg-and-cress sandwiches and warm stout, and he and an uncle and a father sat down on the *Evening Post* until the sea touched their feet.

Prayer Let us spend a moment in silence, thinking about the term (year) which has just passed. Let us remember the moments which have been important to us as individuals, times of worry or anxiety as well as moments of happiness; times when we have learned new skills or something new about the world in which we live; times when we have made new friends and learned something more about getting on with other people. Let us give thanks for these experiences.

Pause.

Lord, as we think of all the activities we have shared together,
    —the new skills we have learned
    —the new friendships we have made
    —the new undertakings we have gained
We give thanks for all that our life together has brought to us.
We offer to you our lives, our work and our holidays, and ask that we may return refreshed ready to learn more of you, and of your world.

Amen.

47

Hymn   Now thank we all our God *or* Lord dismiss us with thy blessing.

Leader   The Lord bless us in the country and at the seaside, at home or abroad,
in our leisure and our work, in school or in a job
in the present and in the future.

Amen.

(c) Christian Aid

A map of Africa, showing the Ethiopian coast line, should be displayed.

Leader   **A song of creation.**

Reader 1 Bless the Lord, my soul!

Readers
1 & 2 Lord God, how great you are,

Readers 1,
2 & 3 clothed in majesty and glory.

Readers 1,
2, 3 & 4 wrapped in light as a robe!

Reader 1 You founded the earth on its base, to stand firm from age to age,
You wrapped it with the ocean like a cloak: the waters stood higher
than the mountains.

Reader 2 At your threat they took to flight; at the voice of your thunder, they fled.
They rose over the mountains and flowed down to the place which
you had appointed.
You set limits they might not pass lest they return to cover the earth.

Reader 3 You make springs gush forth in the valleys; they flow in between the hills.

Reader 1 They give drink to all the beasts of the field; the wild-asses quench
their thirst.

Reader 2 On their banks dwell the birds of heaven; from the branches they
sing their song.

Reader 3 From your dwelling you water the hills; earth drinks its fill of your gifts.

48

Reader 1 You made the moon to mark the months; the sun knows the time for
its setting.

Reader 2 When you spread the darkness it is night and all the beasts of the
forest creep forth.

Reader 3 The young lions roar for their prey and ask their food from God.

Reader 1 At the rising of the sun they steal away and go to rest in their dens.

Reader 2 Man goes forth to his work, to labour till evening falls.

Reader 3 How many are your works, O Lord! In wisdom you have made them all.

Reader 1 The earth is full of your riches.

Reader 2 There is the sea, vast and wide, with its moving swarms past
counting, living things great and small.

Reader 3 The ships are moving there and the monsters you made to play with.

Reader 1 All of these look to you to give them their food in due season.

Readers 1,
 2 & 3 You give it, they gather it up: you open your hand, they have their fill.
(Psalm 103, Gelineau translation)

Leader Today, we shall think particularly of a project in which Christian Aid is
trying to help men reap more food from the sea. Our reading describes a
project in Ethiopia (*point it out on the map*). This plan proposes, not simply
to give food to hungry people, but more important, to show the people
how they themselves can improve their standard of living. The first two
readers describe the coast of Ethiopia and how the people depend on fish,
the third reader describes the project.

Reader 1 The Ethiopian shore-line extends for some 500 nautical miles, and presents
many reefs and bays. These provide both natural shelter, and hazards to
navigation. Off the coast are 360 islands. Winds and currents are very
strong, especially during the monsoon season, making sailing hazardous to
the small, sail-propelled craft.

Reader 2 Dependence on Fish. Most of the shore population, and all the inhabitants of the islands, are completely dependent for their income on the sea. The soil is too poor for the people to earn their living by growing crops or raising cattle.

The most important method of fishing is by seine net from the beach. This produces about 75 per cent of the total catch. Catches include sardines, anchovies and shark. These are dried in the sun and used for the production of fishmeal or for human consumption.

Other methods are gill-netting, fishing by hand-line and cast-net. The total production reaches some 140,000 tons per year. There are, however, so many fishermen working in this way that the amount of fish caught by each fisherman is very low. Fishing craft used are dug-out canoes and two types of sailing boats: over 200 fishing boats are registered.

All these boats are propelled by a single lateen sail, and handled with great skill by the local fishermen.

There are many limitations to this kind of fishing. The boats manœuvre very badly and depend on wind conditions so that often the pursuit of fish schools is almost impossible. Therefore the fishermen use gear which can be operated from the shore. Generally, only schools of fish which approach the shore are caught. When the boats do go out to sea, the catch is often spoiled before it can be delivered because of adverse wind conditions.

Reader 3 The immediate purpose of the project is to increase local fish production by improving the efficiency of local boats and fishing equipment. This will raise the technical and economic level of coastal fishermen in Ethiopia. By adding a motor to the dhows, it would be possible to introduce more efficient and less shore-bound fishing methods, using different and better nets. Christian Aid had been asked to provide a number of suitable engines and a supply of fishing nets. These will be sold to fishermen under a long-term hire-purchase agreement. Because there is only a small market for fresh fish, the project will be directed toward mechanizing those boats chiefly catching fish for the fishmeal industry, where there is a considerable demand for raw material. The income gained from the sale of the engines and fishing gear will form the basis of a fund which will be used to purchase further equipment to help additional fishermen. In this way, one engine or a net will, over the years, benefit a number of fishermen. The project aims finally to motorize all suitable fishing boats in the area and to increase the production of fish by 60 per cent.

Leader Let us Pray.

Lord we give you thanks that we're beginning to grow up.

We're beginning to discover more and more about the treasures of
 your world.
We're beginning to realize that the riches of your world are meant
 to be shared.
We're beginning to understand that 'fair shares for all'
 means not only in this country but throughout the world.

We remember with thanks the work done by Christian Aid,
 Oxfam, the United Nations and organizations like them
 —feeding the hungry
 —caring for the sick
 —giving hope to the hopeless
 —working for peace and understanding
Because of their vision we're beginning to grow up in your world.
Help us to go on working and growing and giving,
Until we have really learned what it means to love our neighbour.

Hymn   Awake, awake to love and work.

(d) The Commonwealth

Commonwealth Day is now celebrated on the Queen's Official Birthday.

The aim of this assembly is to help the idea of the Commonwealth to 'live' in the minds of young people. It should be illustrated by visual aids as much as possible; e.g. a map showing the countries of the Commonwealth should be displayed at the front and large pictures showing cities and citizens of the Commonwealth should also be displayed.

Record   The opening record should be of music or singing from one of the countries of the Commonwealth, *or*

Hymn   Hills of the North, rejoice.

Leader   Today we think particularly of the Commonwealth. The Commonwealth is an association of twenty-six member nations and their dependencies. It is a partnership of countries spread all over the world. Some of these are:

Voice A   *Canada,* a large country on the continent of North America. It is an advanced country. Since it has a sizeable French-speaking population, its two official languages are English and French.

51

Voice B *India,* a large country with a very large and growing population. It is a country of many problems, the main one being to relieve the very great poverty of large numbers of its people. Although many languages are spoken in India, most people follow the Hindu religion.

Voice C *Pakistan,* a country to the north of India, divided into two sections, East and West. Again there is poverty and disease among most of its people. Their main religion is Islam.

Voice D *Australia.* On the other side of the world from Britain, Australia is a large country with proportionately a small population. Australia is probably most famous for its cricket, sheep farming and the 'Flying Doctor' service.

Voice E *Zambia,* a country in Central Africa, which received its independence in 1964. A country of several races, its people are working very hard to make their country more prosperous.

Voice F *Jamaica.* In the Carribean Islands, Jamaica is one of the countries of the West Indies. The people of Jamaica are also of many races and the country has many problems of poverty and education to solve. Its most famous export is sugar and it is also well known for its climate and its cricketers.

At this point it is suggested that any member of the school who comes from one of the Commonwealth countries should be asked to say something about that country; i.e. how large it is in proportion to Britain, what the climate is like, how schools compare with British schools, any particular problem the country faces, etc. Alternatively, slides or a section of film strip supplied by the school's geography department and showing something of life in one of the Commonwealth countries, might be shown.

Voice A It's all very well to think about the Commonwealth on Commonwealth Day, but what's it got to do with ordinary people? Not very much, I should say.

Voice B Perhaps not. But I read somewhere that there are several hundred million people in the Commonwealth, of all sorts and races and coming from very different countries. You can't ignore something as big as that.

Voice C What's more, these countries have joined together in a voluntary friendly association so that they can help each other by sharing their knowledge and resources and even enjoy everyday things together, like sport, music and art. Surely an organization which aims to help people understand each other better is needed in the world today.

Voice A Yes, I suppose that's true. But we've got over a million people from the Commonwealth in Britain now.

Voice B I should think we might learn a lot more about the Commonwealth and what it means if we started with the people from the Commonwealth on our own doorstep and listened to what they had to say to us. We might be very surprised!

Leader Prayer.   Lord, we live in a world
Where there are not fair shares for all.
We spend thousands of pounds a year on chocolates,
While elsewhere, thousands of people die of hunger.

Response Help us to work together for more equal shares in your world.

Leader Lord, we live in a world where people do not understand each other, where there is suspicion and fear.

Response Help us to work together for better understanding in your world.

Leader Lord, we live in a world where we often do not notice our neighbour and we do not know that he can help us and we can help him.

Response Help us to work together for friendship and peace in your world.
Amen.
As the Assembly ends, the record used at the beginning could be repeated or a small group from the school could sing 'All mixed up'.

(e) United Nations

Hymn Thy kingdom come, on bended knee.

Leader Throughout the ages, men of vision have dreamed of the brotherhood of all mankind.

Reader It shall come to pass in the latter days that the mountain of the Lord shall be established as the highest of the mountains, and shall be raised up above the hills; and peoples shall flow to it, and many nations shall come and say.

Voice A Come, let us go up to the mountain of the Lord

Voice B to the house of the God of Jacob;

Voice A that he may teach us his ways

Voice B and we may walk in his paths.

Voice A For out of Zion shall go forth the law,

Voice B and the word of the Lord from Jerusalem.

Voice A He shall judge between many peoples,

Voice B and shall decide for strong nations afar off;

Voice A and they shall beat their swords into plough-shares,

Voice B and their spears into pruning hooks;

Voice A nation shall not lift up sword against nation,

Voice B neither shall they learn war any more.

(Micah 4: 1-3)

Leader The Charter of the United Nations was drawn up in 1945 after the world had been shattered by two major wars within thirty years. The Charter itself begins with this statement:
'We, the Peoples of the United Nations, determined to save succeeding generations from the scourge of war, which twice in our lifetime has brought untold sorrow to mankind, and to reaffirm faith in fundamental human rights, in the dignity and worth of the human person, in the equal rights of men and women and of nations large and small,
and to establish conditions under which justice and respect for the obligations arising from treaties and other sources of international law can be maintained, and to promote social progress and better standards of life in larger freedom,
and for these ends
to practise tolerance and live together in peace with one another as good neighbours,
and to unite our strength
to maintain international peace and security,
and to ensure, by the acceptance of principles and the institution of

methods, that armed force shall not be used, save in the common interest, and to employ international machinery for the promotion of the economic and social advancement of all peoples,
have resolved to combine our efforts to accomplish these aims.'

Leader Prayers.
Because the leaders of the world now meet around the conference table
    to try to work together,
    to try to understand each other,
    to try to help each other,

Response We thank you Lord.

Leader Because we're beginning to understand that all men wherever they are, are human beings like ourselves
    with needs like ours,
    with worries like ours,
    with cares like ours,

Response We thank you Lord.

Leader Because through the United Nations Agencies men are working together
    to share medical knowledge,
    to increase the production of food,
    to care for those who suffer,

Response We thank you Lord.

Leader This is your world, Lord, the world you love:

Response Help us to live responsibly in it . . .

Leader In the twentieth century you have opened to us the gate of knowledge, you have enabled us to conquer space and distance, you have given us power over life and death:

Response Help us to use our knowledge and power for the good of mankind.

Leader In the cry of hungry children, in the faces of homeless refugees, in the loneliness of old people, in the outstretched arms of the imprisoned and the oppressed:

Response Help us to see and hear you, and to respond with love and justice.

Leader In all the places where men struggle for conquest, by words or by weapons; in all the places where men surround themselves by high walls of hatred, fear, and prejudice; in all the places where the human family is divided by the selfishness and weakness of its members; and in all the moments of our own frailty and failure;

Response Help us to know what you are saying to us, and give us the courage and strength to obey.

Leader Jesus the liberator, forever opening the doors that imprison people in body, mind, and spirit:

Response Set us free to serve you; help us to set others free; and may your freedom, love, and truth be known by all people everywhere.

Amen.

Hymn God is working his purpose out.

Leader We are free to serve. Let us go in peace.

Everybody
> The Spirit of the Lord is upon us because he has anointed us;
> He has sent us to announce good news to the poor,
> To proclaim release for prisoners and recovery of sight for the blind;
> To let the broken victims go free,
> To proclaim the year of the Lord's favour.
> So be it!

Sources:
The Voices on pages 43–45 are from Michel Quoist, *Prayers of Life*, Gill and Macmillan.
The reading on pages 46–47 is from Dylan Thomas, *Portrait of the Artist as a Young Dog*, Dent and Sons.

5 ADVENT AND CHRISTMAS

(a) The coming of hope

Hymn   Hark the glad sound.

Reader 1 Luke 1: 26–35.

Reader 2 **Christmas.**

The bells of waiting Advent ring,
   The Tortoise stove is lit again
And lamp-oil light across the night
   Has caught the streaks of winter rain
In many a stained-glass window sheen
From Crimson Lake to Hooker's Green.

The holly in the windy hedge
   And round the Manor House the yew
Will soon be stripped to deck the ledge,
   The altar, font and arch and pew,
So that the villagers can say
'The church looks nice' on Christmas Day.

Provincial public houses blaze
   And Corporation tramcars clang,
On lighted tenements I gaze
   Where paper decorations hang,
And bunting in the red Town Hall
Says 'Merry Christmas to you all'.

And London shops on Christmas Eve
   Are strung with silver bells and flowers
As hurrying clerks the City leave
   To pigeon-haunted classic towers,
And marbled clouds go scudding by
The many-steepled London sky.

57

And girls in slacks remember Dad,
    And oafish louts remember Mum,
And sleepless children's hearts are glad,
    And Christmas-morning bells say 'Come!'
Even to shining ones who dwell
Safe in the Dorchester Hotel.

And is it true? And is it true,
    This most tremendous tale of all,
Seen in a stained-glass window's hue,
    A Baby in an Ox's stall?
The Maker of the stars and sea
Become a Child on earth for me?

And is it true? For if it is,
    No loving fingers tying strings
Around those tissued fripperies,
    The sweet and silly Christmas things,
Bath salts and inexpensive scent
And hideous tie so kindly meant,

No love that in a family dwells,
    No carolling in frosty air,
Nor all the steeple-shaking bells
    Can with this single Truth compare—
That God was Man in Palestine
And lives today in Bread and Wine.

Leader   Let us pray.
Lord, when you came to the world you brought us hope,
When you came to our darkness you brought us light,
When you came to our strife you brought us peace.
Now, as Christmas approaches we again think of your coming.
Help us to turn the hope
                        the light
                        and the peace
Which you brought us into reality in today's world.
                                            Amen.

Song   Every man neath his vine and fig tree.
        or
Hymn   The race that long in darkness pined.

58

(b) The joy of Christmas

Carol Angels, from the realms of glory.

Leader A man discovers the joy and the spirit of Christmas. The next two readings are from *A Christmas Carol* by Charles Dickens. The first shows Scrooge, the old, unhappy miser, the central figure in the story. He is described as 'a squeezing, wrenching, grasping, scraping, clutching, covetous old sinner'. On Christmas Eve a visitor comes to him in his business house.

Reader 1 'At this festive season of the year, Mr. Scrooge,' said the gentleman, taking up a pen, 'it is more than usually desirable that we should make some slight provision for the poor and destitute, who suffer greatly at the present time. Many thousands are in want of common necessaries; hundreds of thousands are in want of common comforts, sir.'
'Are there no prisons?' asked Scrooge.
'Plenty of prisons,' said the gentleman, laying down the pen again.
'And the Union workhouses?' demanded Scrooge. 'Are they still in operation?'
'They are. Still,' returned the gentleman, 'I wish I could say they were not.'
'The Treadmill and the Poor Law are in full vigour, then?' said Scrooge.
'Both very busy, sir.'
'Oh! I was afraid, from what you said at first that something had occurred to stop them in their useful course,' said Scrooge. 'I'm very glad to hear it.'
'Under the impression that they scarcely furnish Christian cheer of mind or body to the multitude,' returned the gentleman, 'a few of us are endeavouring to raise a fund to buy the Poor some meat and drink, and means of warmth. We choose this time because it is a time, of all others, when Want is keenly felt, and Abundance rejoices. What shall I put you down for?'
'Nothing!' Scrooge replied.
'You wish to be anonymous?'
'I wish to be left alone,' said Scrooge. 'Since you ask me what I wish, gentleman, that is my answer. I don't make merry myself at Christmas, and I can't afford to make idle people merry. I help to support the establishments I have mentioned: they cost enough: and those who are badly off must go there.'
'Many can't go there; and many would rather die.'
'If they would rather die,' said Scrooge, 'they had better do it, and decrease the surplus population.'

Leader   During the night of Christmas Eve the story tells how Scrooge had a dream
in which spirits visited him and showed him in a very dramatic way how
his mean and miserly way of life had produced great unhappiness and suffering, not only in his own life but also in the lives of those who came into
contact with him. This included his relatives, but chiefly concerned Bob
Cratchit, the clerk who worked long hours for low wages and whose
family was extremely poor. At the end of his dream Scrooge, very shaken
by what the spirits had shown him, resolved that he would alter his life
and try to make amends for the past.

The next reading describes him as he awoke.

Reader 2 'I don't know what to do!' cried Scrooge, laughing and crying in the same
breath. 'I am as light as a feather, I am as happy as an angel, I am as
merry as a school-boy. I am as giddy as a drunken man. A Merry Christmas to everybody! A Happy New Year to all the world. Hallo here!
Whoop! Hallo!'

'I don't know what day of the month it is!' said Scrooge. 'I don't know
how long I've been among the spirits. I don't know anything. I'm quite
a baby. Never mind. I don't care. I'd rather be a baby. Hallo! Whoop!
Hallo here!'

He was checked in his transports by the churches ringing out the lustiest
peals he had ever heard. Clash, bang, hammer, ding, dong, bell. Bell,
dong, ding, hammer, clang, clash! Oh glorious, glorious!

Running to the window he opened it, and put out his head. No fog, no
mist; clear, bright, jovial, stirring, cold; cold, piping for the blood to
dance to; golden sunlight; heavenly sky; sweet fresh air; merry bells. Oh,
glorious. Glorious!

'What's today, my fine fellow?' said Scrooge.

'Today!' replied the boy. 'Why, Christmas Day.'

'It's Christmas Day!' said Scrooge to himself. I haven't missed it. The
spirits have done it all in one night. They can do anything they like. Of
course they can. Of course they can.

'Hallo, my fine fellow!'

'Hallo!' returned the boy.

'Do you know the poulterer's in the next street but one, at the corner?'
Scrooge inquired.

'I should hope I did,' replied the lad.

'An intelligent boy!' said Scrooge. 'A remarkable boy! Do you know
whether they've sold the prize turkey that was hanging up there? Not the
little prize turkey: the big one?'

'What, the one as big as me?' returned the boy.

'What a delightful boy!' said Scrooge. 'It's a pleasure to talk to him. Yes, my buck!'

'It's hanging there now,' replied the boy.

'Is it?' said Scrooge. 'Go and buy it.'

'Walk-ER!' exclaimed the boy.

'No, no,' said Scrooge, 'I am in earnest. Go and buy it, and tell 'em to bring it here, that I may give them the direction where to take it. Come back with the man, and I'll give you a shilling. Come back with him in less than five minutes, and I'll give you half-a-crown!'

The boy was off like a shot.

'I'll send it to Bob Cratchit's!' whispered Scrooge, rubbing his hands, and splitting with a laugh. 'He shan't know who sends it. It's twice the size of Tiny Tim.'

The hand in which he wrote the address was not a steady one, but write it he did, somehow, and went downstairs to open the street door, ready for the coming of the poulterer's man.

It *was* a turkey! He could never have stood upon his legs, that bird. He would have snapped 'em short off in a minute, like sticks of sealing-wax. 'Why, it's impossible to carry that to Camden Town', said Scrooge. 'You must have a cab.'

The chuckle with which he said this, and the chuckle with which he paid for the turkey, and the chuckle with which he paid for the cab, and the chuckle with which he recompensed the boy, were only to be exceeded by the chuckle with which he sat down breathless in his chair again, and chuckled till he cried.

Shaving was not an easy task, for his hand continued to shake very much; and shaving requires attention, even when you don't dance while you are at it. But if he had cut the end of his nose off, he would have put a piece of sticking-plaster over it, and been quite satisfied.

He dressed himself 'all in his best', and at last got out into the streets. The people were by this time pouring forth, as he had seen them with the Ghost of Christmas Present; and walking with his hands behind him, Scrooge regarded everyone with a delighted smile. He looked so irresistibly pleasant, in a word, that three or four good-humoured fellows said 'Good morning, sir. A Merry Christmas to you!'

And Scrooge said often afterwards, that of all the blithe sounds he had ever heard, those were the blithest in his ears.

Preferably these two episodes should be presented dramatically by pupils.

Reading Luke 2: 8–14.

Carol   Hark! the herald-angels sing.

Prayers These days, we're so busy making plans for Christmas!
We rush from one crowded shop to another, trying to find a scarf
   of just the right colour, for an aunt we'd almost forgotten!
We spend hours putting up the decorations
      the holly and mistletoe in the hall,
      Christmas cards strung round the room,
      paper chains and tinsel round the fireplace.
Mum spends her time planning the meals and ordering food,
And Dad spends his time wondering what on earth to get for Mum!
Excitedly we rush to the door when the postman comes
   only to discover we must dash to the shops once more to
   buy a card for someone else we'd almost forgotten!
Lord, let us not be so busy that we lose sight of the meaning behind it all.
Help us to find true joy, in all the moments these exciting days of
                        Christmas bring to us.
And though we think of joy and goodwill especially at Christmas,
Help us to know that your spirit is with us always, and to live our
                        lives in that Spirit.
                        Amen.

(c) Gifts

During the Christmas season, schools often make collections to give to worthwhile causes. These collections can take several forms; money for charity; gifts for the handicapped or elderly; books for the Ranfurly Library Scheme, etc. This assembly assumes that such a collection has taken place in the school and the offering of these gifts is central to it.

Carol   As with gladness men of old.

Leader One of the things we think about at Christmastime is the joy of giving and receiving presents. Our first reading is part of an account of Christmas written by a Welsh poet. He looked back on his childhood and recalled what a magical, exciting time it was. This section of the account, which takes the form of a conversation between two boys, is about presents.

Voice A Get them back to the postmen.

Voice B They were just ordinary postmen, fond of walking and dogs and Christmas and the snow.
They knocked on the doors with blue knuckles . . .

Voice A Ours has got a black knocker . . .

Voice B And then they stood on the white Welcome mat in the little, drifted porches and huffed and puffed, making ghosts with their breath, and jogged from foot to foot like small boys wanting to go out.

Voice A And then the Presents?

Voice B And then the Presents, after the Christmas box. And the cold postman, with a rose on his button-nose, tingled down the tea-tray-slithered run of the chilly glinting hill. He went in his ice-bound boots like a man on fish-monger's slabs. He wagged his bag like a frozen camel's hump, dizzily turned the corner on one foot, and, by God, he was gone.

Voice A Get back to the Presents.

Voice B There were the Useful Presents: engulfing mufflers of the old coach days, and mittens made for giant sloths; zebra scarfs of a substance like silky gum that could be tug-o'-warred down to the goloshes; blinding tam-o'-shanters like patchwork tea cosies and bunny-suited busbies and balaclavas for victims of head-shrinking tribes; from aunts who always wore wool next to the skin there were moustached and rasping vests that made you wonder why the aunts had any skin left at all; and once I had a little crocheted nose bag from an aunt now, alas, no longer whinnying with us. And pictureless books in which small boys, though warned with quotations not to, *would* skate on Farmer Giles' pond and did and drowned; and books that told me everything about the wasp, except why.

Voice A Go on to the Useless Presents.

Voice B Bags of moist and many-coloured jelly babies and a folded flag and a false nose and a tram-conductor's cap and a machine that punched tickets and rang a bell; never a catapult; once, by mistake that no one could explain, a little hatchet; and a celluloid duck that made, when you pressed it, a most unducklike sound.
And a packet of cigarettes: you put one in your mouth and you stood at the corner of the street and you waited for hours, in vain, for an old lady to

scold you for smoking a cigarette, and then you ate it. And then it was breakfast under the balloons.

Reader   God's greatest gift to man.   Luke 2: 1–7.

Reader   Men bring their gifts to the infant Jesus.   Matthew 2: 1–12a.

Carol   Brightest and best of the sons of the morning.
> *During the singing of this carol, representatives of each class, carrying the gifts which have been collected, or tokens of them, should move to the front or central point of the assembly, placing them on a table.*

Leader   Prayers.
Because we know that there are those in the world whose needs are greater than ours,

All   Lord, we offer our gifts.

Leader   Because we know of many who long for so many material things we take for granted,

All   Lord, we offer our gifts.

Leader   Because we know of the need of all men for our care and our love,

All   Lord, we offer our gifts.

Leader   Because at Christmastime we think especially of your greatest gift to us,

All   Lord, we offer our gifts. Use them and use us to bring your joy, your peace and your love into the world this Christmas time and throughout the coming year.

Leader   Let us say the grace together.

All   May the grace of our Lord Jesus Christ
and the love of God
and the fellowship of the Holy Spirit
be with us now and always.
Amen.

Record   For unto us a child is born (Handel's *Messiah*).
        During this record, the assembly disperses.

(d) The Prince of Peace

Record   Glory to God (Handel's *Messiah*).

Reader 1 The voice of a prophet. Isaiah 2: 2–4.

Reader 2 The world of today. A hospital in wartime.
        I got an interpreter and went round the wards asking plain factual
        questions. The old are pitiful in their bewilderment, the adults seem
        locked in an aloof resignation, the children's ward is unbearable. No one
        protests or complains. We big overfed white people will never know what
        they feel.
        A boy of 15 sat on his cot with both legs in plaster casts. He and his little
        brother had gone to the beach to mend nets; a Vietnamese patrol boat
        saw them and opened up with machine gun fire; his little brother was
        killed. The boat then pulled in to shore to see what it had bagged and
        found two children. The American adviser got the living boy to the
        nearest town, where a helicopter picked him up. His mother and older
        brother made their way here by motor-boat to nurse him. He is lucky;
        he has only been in this appalling place for two and a half months and will
        some day walk again. He said he did not know the beach was forbidden;
        that was his only comment.

Reader 3 The voice of a prophet. Isaiah 9: 2, 6, 7.

Reader 4 The world of today. Orphans in wartime.
        There are ten children's orphanages in Saigon alone, and orphanages
        throughout the country, and no reason to think that each does not receive
        its terrible quota of newly-born and starving. In another suburb, in an
        orphanage for 675 children, a gentle barefooted Vietnamese nun showed
        me their crowded babies' ward. By local standards this is a wonderful
        orphanage because, helped by foreign charities, it can provide some
        modern medical care.
        In Soeur Jeanne's crèche, beyond the cots of the babies, small children
        crawled on the floor, or sat with outstretched legs, or stood alone; all thin,
        all silent, all with dark, sad eyes. Soeur Jeanne said, 'The misery, the
        misery. Everything is here. War orphans. War wounded. Tubercular.

Crippled by polio. Deaf and dumb. Blind. Children of lepers. Children of refugees who cannot feed them. Men do not see the real misery of war. They do not wish to. Why don't they do something for the poor people of Saigon? It cannot go on like this.'

But it never stops. Officially, 80,000 orphans are registered now, which means in institutions, and an institution is the last desperate resort. The Vietnamese exist as all-inclusive families, and they love children. No one could guess how many orphans are sheltered by relatives. The Ministry of Social Welfare predicts an average of 2,000 more orphans every month. Is it not strange that we count and proclaim only military casualties? These homeless children should be listed as wounded; and wounded ever.

Reader 5 The voice of a prophet. Isaiah 11 : 6, 7, 9.

Reader 6 The world of today. Refugees in wartime.

Again we tiptoed through broken shards of china, tin cans, mounds of indecipherable refuse. 'Mosquitoes?' I asked, noting the tracts of green water. No one took the point. 'A US civilian medic team comes once a week,' Tri reported; 'the camp leader says the biggest sickness is diarrhoea'. From which babies here often die. 'And the people are underfed.'

We stopped at the first miserable shack because I could not bear to walk further. It was about eight by ten feet in size, nearly filled by two beds, reeking of poverty, with dingy rags of clothing hung on nails, and the battered household goods on a narrow shelf. A woman, who looked 55 was perhaps 35, drained, exhausted, gaunt, lived here with seven children and her husband. By trade, he repaired clocks and watches, but was ill and, besides, could find no work.

Three young children lay on the bare boards of the beds, silently; yes, they were sick. She didn't know what their sickness was, but she could not give them enough to eat. Only her teenage daughter had a job, miles away. 'Maybe two hours to go there, two hours to come home,' Tri said. The girl earned 80 piastres a day, 48 US cents, three shillings and threepence, the entire income for the family. Occasionally, food is distributed by the Catholic charities, otherwise there is no direct aid. 'How will she ever get one of the cement houses?' I asked. 'She says she hopes the priest will help her.'

Reader 7 The Prince of peace comes to a world of strife. Luke 2: 8–14.

Carol It came upon a midnight clear.

Leader Let us pray.
Somewhere in the world today men are fighting each other.
For thousands of years the prophets have dreamed of peace on earth.
At Christmas time we think particularly of peace on earth.
Help us to work for it.
We think of all those who in this world are suffering in body,
   mind and spirit because of war and man's inhumanity to man
 —mothers and children
 —the orphaned and the elderly, who have lost their homes,
   their health and their sanity.
Help us always to remember them
   to work for them and to work for peace in your world.
Lord, make us instruments of your peace
 Where there is hatred, let us sow love;
 Where there is injury, pardon;
 Where there is discord, union;
 Where there is doubt, faith;
 Where there is despair, hope;
 Where there is darkness, light;
 Where there is sadness, joy;
   for your mercy and your truth's sake.
           Amen.

Record Glory to God.
  During this record the assembly disperses.

(e) Christ comes to man

Carol O little town of Bethlehem.

Reader The birth of Jesus. Matthew 1: 18–25.

Reader The word became flesh; he came to dwell among us, and we saw his glory such glory as befits the Father's only son, full of grace and truth.

Leader To put the story of Christmas at its simplest, you could say 'Christ came to men'. At Christmas time in particular, we remember and celebrate his coming. We shall now listen to (watch) a story which shows what Christ's coming to men means for us today.

Although the following reading is presented in story form it should preferably be presented as a short play. Alternatively it could be read dramatically with different pupils reading the words spoken by Martin and his visitors, etc.

Story Christ Comes to Man.

In a certain town there lived a shoemaker named Martin Avdeitch. He lived in a basement room which possessed but one window. This window looked onto the street, and through it a glimpse could be caught of the passers-by. It is true that only their legs could be seen, but that did not matter, as Martin could recognize people by their boots alone. He had lived here for a long time, and so had many acquaintances. There were very few pairs of boots in the neighbourhood which had not passed through his hands at least once, if not twice. Some he had re-soled, others he had fitted with side-pieces, others again, he had resewn where they were split, or provided with new toe-caps. Yes, he often saw his handiwork through that window. He was given plenty of custom, for his work lasted well, his materials were good, his prices moderate, and his word to be depended on. One night while he was reading his Bible, he fell asleep. Suddenly he seemed to hear the voice of Christ saying, 'Martin, Martin! Look thou into the street tomorrow, for I am coming to visit thee.' Martin roused himself, got up from the chair, and rubbed his eyes. He did not know whether it was dreaming or awake that he had heard these words, but he turned out the lamp and went to bed.

The next morning Avdeitch rose before daylight and said his prayers. Then he made up the stove, got ready some cabbage soup and porridge, slung his leather apron about him, and sat down to his work in the window. He sat and worked hard, and as he worked he kept looking out of the window as much as working. Whenever a pair of boots passed with which he was acquainted he would bend down to glance upwards through the window and see their owner's face as well. The doorkeeper passed in new felt boots, and then a water-carrier. Next, an old soldier, a ve teran of Nicholas army, in old, patched boots, and carrying a shovel inhis hands, halted' close by the window. Avdeitch knew him by his boots. His name was Stepanitch, and he was kept by a neighbouring tradesman out of charity, his duties being to help the doorkeeper. He began to clear away the snow from in front of Avdeitch's window, while the shoemaker looked at him and then resumed his work.

After a while, Martin brewed some tea, and then tapped with his finger on the window-pane. Stepanitch turned round and approached. Avdeitch beckoned to him, and then went to open the door.

'Come in and warm yourself,' he said. 'You must be frozen.'

'Christ requite you!' answered Stepanitch. 'Yes, my bones are almost cracking.'

So Martin welcomed Stepanitch into his home for a while, cheering him with hot tea and conversation. When Stepanitch had gone, Martin returned to his work.

Two soldiers passed the window, the one in military boots, and the other in civilian. Next, there came a neighbouring householder, in polished goloshes; then a baker with a basket. All of them passed on. Presently a woman in woollen stockings and rough country shoes approached the window, and halted near the buttress outside it. Avdeitch peered up at her from under the lintel of his window, and could see that she was a plain-looking, poorly-dressed woman and had a child in her arms.

Avdeitch rose, went to the door, climbed the steps, and cried out, 'My good woman, my good woman!'

She heard him and turned round.

'Why need you stand there in the cold with your baby?' he went on. 'Come into my room, where it is warm, and where you will be able to wrap the baby up more comfortably than you can do here. Yes, come in with you.'

The woman was surprised to see an old man in a leather apron and with spectacles upon his nose calling out to her, yet she followed him down the steps, and they entered his room. The old man led her to the bedstead.

'Sit you down here, my good woman,' he said. 'You will be near the stove, and can warm yourself and feed your baby.'

While Martin gave hot soup to the woman and her child she told him who she was. He learned that she was the wife of a soldier who had been away for some time. She was so poor that she had even had to pawn her shawl to buy food for her child and herself. She had been looking for work but had been unable to find any. Martin rummaged in a cupboard and produced an old jacket.

'Here,' he said. 'It is a poor old thing, but it will serve to cover you.'

The woman was overcome with gratitude. When, after they had talked together for a little longer, the woman came to leave, Martin gave her a little money with which to buy herself a shawl. He returned to his work, carefully watching the window to see who was passing. Although a certain number of people did pass by, there was never anyone very particular.

Suddenly, he saw something. There was a scuffle going on outside and he saw that a boy had tried to steal an apple from a pedlar-woman's basket. Martin rushed outside to where the woman was holding the boy by the hair, trying to beat him, while the boy, protesting his innocence, was trying to escape. Martin did his best to try to separate them and eventually persuaded the boy to ask the woman's pardon. He suggested to the woman that she should forgive the boy.

'That's all very well,' she said 'but these young rascals are so spoilt already!'

'Then it's for us, their elders, to teach them better,' replied Martin.

After talking a little more she did forgive the boy, and he feeling really sorry for what he had done, offered to carry her firewood. As they walked together down the street, Martin watched them go. By this time it was evening, so he went indoors and began to clear away his work. He lit the lamp and took down his Bible from the shelf. He had intended opening the book at the place which he had marked last night with a strip of leather, but it opened itself at another instead. The instant it did so, his vision of last night came back to his memory, and, as instantly, he thought he heard a movement behind him as of someone moving towards him. He looked round and saw in the shadow of a dark corner what appeared to be figures —figures of persons standing there, yet could not distinguish them clearly. Then the voice whispered in his ear:

'Martin, Martin, dost thou not know me?'

'Who art thou?' said Avdeitch.

'Even I!' whispered the voice again. 'Lo, it is I!'—and there stepped from the dark corner Stepanitch. He smiled, and then, like the fading of a little cloud, was gone.

'It is I!' whispered the voice again—and there stepped from the same corner the woman with her baby. She smiled, and the baby smiled, and they were gone.

'And it is I!' whispered the voice again—and there stepped forth the old woman and the boy with the apple. They smiled and were gone.

Joy filled the soul of Martin Avdeitch as he put on his spectacles, and set himself to read the Testament at the place where it had opened. At the top of the page he read:

'For I was an hungered, and ye gave me meat: I was thirsty, and ye gave me drink: I was a stranger, and ye took me in.'

And further down the page he read:

'Inasmuch as ye have done it unto one of the least of these my brethren ye have done it unto me.'

Then Avdeitch understood that the vision had come true, and that his Saviour had in very truth visited him that day, and that he had received him.

Leader Prayers.

At Christmas time we remember that you came to men.

Response Lord, we offer thanks and praise.

Leader　With your coming, you shewed us the meaning of love, joy and truth.

Response Lord, we offer thanks and praise.

Leader　With your coming, you shewed us that the power of love can transform our lives and transform the world.

Response Lord, we offer thanks and praise.

Leader　Lord, we ask you to be with us this Christmas time
　　　　　in our hopes and expectations
　　　　　in our giving and receiving
　　　　　in our work and relaxation
　　　　　in our noisy celebrations and quiet moments
　　　　　among our families and friends.
Be with us and help us to recognize that you are with us always, calling us to respond to you in service to our fellow men.

Amen.

Sources:
The poem on pages 57–58 is by John Betjeman, from *Collected Poems*, published by John Murray.
The Voices on pages 62–64 are from Dylan Thomas, *A Child's Christmas in Wales*, Dent and Sons.
Readers 2, 4 and 6 on pages 65–66 are from Martha Gellhorn, *A New Kind of War*, Sphere Books.
The story on pages 68–70 is from L. Tolstoy, *Master and Man*, Everyman.

6 LENT AND EASTER

(a) A true Lent

Reader 1 Matthew 4: 1–10.

Leader On Ash Wednesday, we traditionally think of the temptation of Jesus. This begins the period in the church's calendar known as Lent. As Jesus was in the wilderness for forty days, so Lent lasts for forty days and in our calendar leads to Easter. Most people associate Lent with fasting or giving up some luxury in our lives. Today we shall think about the meaning of Lent. First, a poem in which the writer tries to examine the question of what a Lenten fast means and what kind of fast it should be.

Reader 2 Is this a Fast, to keep
                    The Larder leane?
                        And cleane
From fat of Veales and Sheep?

Is it to quit the dish
                    Of Flesh, yet still
                        To fill
The platter high with Fish?

Is it to faste an houre,
                    Or rag'd to go,
                        Or show
A downcast look, and sowre.

No: 'tis a Fast, to dole
                    Thy sheaf of wheat
                        And meat
Unto the hungry soule.

It is to fast from strife,
                    From old debate,
                        And hate;

72

To circumcize thy life.

To shew a heart grief-rent;
                    To starve thy sin,
                        Not Bin;
And that's to keep thy Lent.

Leader   A true Lent, says the poet, is to give wheat and meat to the hungry soul. Rather than think of Lent simply as a time of discipline and giving up something, we should consider the deeper meaning. This is to give wheat and meat to the hungry soul and to give up strife and hate.

Song   Judas and Mary (or Record).

Leader   Lord, as we remember your temptation
help us to overcome our temptations to greed and selfishness.
Help us to love and serve you whom we meet in the poor and needy of the earth.
          Amen.

(b) What hate can do

Leader   A psalm by a boy aged thirteen.

Voice A   Man has great power. He has conquered the earth, the heavens and the oceans. But he has not conquered his hatred and jealousy over others.

Voice B   Man kills and destroys his own kind and the wonders you have created.

Voice A   Man hates his own kind for a different colour and faith.

Voice B   Why did you create man with a brain? Why did you not leave him like the creatures he is now destroying because of his brain?

Voice A   Without a brain man would be limited, so many would not starve and die.

Voice B   There would be a better earth if man had not a great brain, to inspire hatred and victory for himself alone.

Voice A   Many men these days of course are good, but even they are not perfect.

Voice B They have a spark of hatred for others hidden in their mighty brain.

Leader During wartime, a young boy hates his enemies automatically:

Reader One winter evening my uncles came home from the taiga (forest). They drank and made a noise half through the night, their beery voices singing songs as slow and never-ending as Russian rivers. Finally they put out the lights and went to bed.
I went out on to the porch in my pants and slippers for a drink of water and stumbled against something which gave off a strange booming sound. Fumbling in the darkness for a box of matches, I saw by their uncertain light, piled one upon another, the bodies of roe-deer made hard and resonant by the forty-degree frost. Their legs pointed at the roof. Their large eyes gazed at me with a questioning, human look. As though hypnotized, I sat down on my bare knees on the rime-covered floor and pressed myself against their icy bodies, trying to move them this way and that. I tried breathing on them. At first I thought they were only frozen, then I saw a small spot of blood on the delicate, childlike forehead of one of them.
Hugging it, I burst into bitter sobs.
My uncles woke up and came rushing out. They pulled me away with difficulty and were quite unable to understand why it took me so long afterwards to calm down.
It was indeed hard to understand why any boy should weep over the bodies of roe-deer at a time when so much human blood was being shed.
I myself, when I heard the news from the front over the radio, rejoiced at the number of Germans who had been killed, though I wept over the deer. I could not see the Germans as human beings.
They were the enemies.

Leader In the story of Easter, we read how hatred tried to conquer love.

Reader Luke 22: 1–6; 23: 13–25.

Prayer You came to earth to bring us true life and men put you to death.
You taught us the way of love and men responded with hate.
How long will it take us to learn, Lord?
For nearly two thousand years we have gone on
      with our selfishness,
      our fighting,
      and our hatred.

74

And the world is so full of so much suffering and needs so much love.
Help us to understand your way of love and build our lives upon it.
O Lord, teach us to love and not to hate.

Hymn   My song is love unknown.

(c) Forgiveness

Hymn   At the name of Jesus.

Reader 1 As they led him away to execution they seized upon a man called Simon, from Cyrene, on his way in from the country, put the cross on his back, and made him walk behind Jesus carrying it. There were two others with him, criminals who were being led away to execution; and when they reached the place called The Skull, they crucified him there, and the criminals with him, one on his right and the other on his left. Jesus said, 'Father, forgive them; they do not know what they are doing.'

Reader 2 **A Russian Poet Writes of his Boyhood.**
In 1941, Mama took me back to Moscow. There I saw our enemy for the first time. If my memory is right, nearly 20,000 German war prisoners were to be marched in a single column through the streets of Moscow.
The pavements swarmed with onlookers, cordoned off by soldiers and police. The crowd were mostly women—Russian women with hands roughened by hard work, lips untouched by lipstick and thin hunched shoulders which had borne half the burden of the war. Every one of them must have had a father or a husband, a brother or a son killed by the Germans.
They gazed with hatred in the direction from which the column was to appear. At last we saw it.
The generals marched at the head, massive chins stuck out, lips folded disdainfully, their whole demeanour meant to show superiority over their plebeian victors . . .
The women were clenching their fists. The soldiers and policemen had all they could do to hold them back.
All at once something happened to them.
They saw German soldiers, thin, unshaven, wearing dirty, bloodstained bandages, hobbling on crutches or leaning on the shoulders of their comrades; the soldiers walked with their heads down.
The street became dead silent—the only sound was the shuffling of boots and the thumping of crutches.

Then I saw an elderly woman in broken-down boots push herself forward and touch a policeman's shoulder, saying, 'Let me through.' There must have been something about her that made him step aside.

She went up to the column, took from inside her coat something wrapped in a coloured handkerchief and unfolded it. It was a crust of black bread. She pushed it awkwardly into the pocket of a soldier, so exhausted that he was tottering on his feet. And now suddenly from every side women were running towards the soldiers, pushing into their hands, bread, cigarettes, whatever they had.

The soldiers were no longer enemies. They were people.

Leader Let us pray.

Lord, I know what it is to feel betrayed.
I placed my trust in someone and he let me down.
He was my friend, and I never believed he could do it.
And now he lives his life, and I live mine.
We never meet and we never speak
I live my life not just as if I hate him, but more, ignoring him,
                                          just as if he didn't exist,
And inside I still carry the pain of the discovery that I was betrayed.
We were very good friends, Lord, and we had so much in common
But since he betrayed my trust, somehow something has gone out
                                          of my life.

Lord, you were betrayed.
The very people to whom you committed your life in the end betrayed you.
But you managed to forgive them
And you loved them till the end, and you taught your followers to
                                          do the same.

If I really think about it
I don't really want to live in a world built on hate.
I want to live in a world which is built on love
    and this means accepting people as they are,
    even when they have wronged us.
Help me to work it out in my life, Lord,
So that I can re-establish contact with my friend,
    so that we can accept each other again.
                              Amen.

Hymn Thine be the glory, risen, conquering Son.

76

(d) Triumph

Hymn   Jesus Christ is risen *or* Jesus Christ is risen today.

Leader   As we come to rejoice in the triumph of Easter, we shall first listen to three readings which are about the personal triumphs which we encounter in our lives.

Reader 1 **A Boy Reads for the First Time.**
On the sewing machine lay Jack's library book, a dirty brown object disguised in a uniform binding with gilt numbers on the back. I picked it up, opened it at the first page, and began to read *The Swiss Family Robinson*. It is an understatement to say that I began to read. I stepped into another life. I was one of that family on the wrecked ship passing through the barrier of words, enlarging my small suburban existence by this new dimension. I could not know what was happening, or the scope of this vast inheritance. I heard the sea breaking on the shore of that fortunate island and I shared with Fritz, Ernest, Jack and Franz in establishing ourselves under the palm trees, and in offering up thanksgiving for our safety. I have never lost that island.
Mother found me sitting at the table, with the book in front of me, and my breathing body in front of the book. Then Jack followed her, and both of them stood watching for some moments before I jerked my head, saw them, and broke the spell.
'I can read,' I said.
Jack frowned; and his frown was always an intimidation. He stepped forward and looked over my shoulder. 'Twenty-five pages!' he said, turning to Mother. 'Now read a bit more. Read it aloud,' he commanded. I read a few sentences, without stumbling.

Reader 2 **A Russian Writer Tells of a Surprise Triumph.**
I was fifteen.
I wanted to become a man and stand on my own feet.
At that time my father was in charge of a geological expedition. When I arrived, ragged and skinny, he looked me over and said: 'So you want to stand on your own feet . . . Well, if you really do, no one here must know you are my son. Otherwise, they'll try to spare you in your work, whether they mean to or not, and that isn't going to make a man of you.'
I joined the expedition as a labourer.
I learned to break the ground with a pick, to knock samples as flat as my

hand from the rock with a hammer, to split the only match we had left in three with a razor blade, and to light a fire in the rain.

I couldn't swim and I lived in fear of being found out and disgraced.

One day I was walking with a geologist along a narrow mountain path above a noisy stream. We both carried rucksacks filled with samples of rock. Suddenly the geologist took a false step and the ground under his feet gave way. He clutched desperately at a bush, missed it and fell headlong from the steep bank into the river below. Within seconds I saw him thrashing about in the foaming water, struggling to keep afloat, but his rucksack was pulling him down.

I flung mine off my shoulders, whipped my knife from inside my belt and jumped in.

It was not until I had swum up to the geologist, cut the straps of his rucksack, and we had both scrambled ashore that I remembered I hadn't learnt to swim.

Reader 3 **Triumph over Fear.**

My education was left to the street. The street taught me to swear, smoke, spit elegantly through my teeth, and to keep my fists at the ready—a habit I have to this day.

I realized that what mattered in the struggle for life was to overcome my fear of those who were stronger.

The ruler of our street . . . was a boy of about sixteen who was nicknamed Red.

Red was big and broad-shouldered beyond his years. Red walked masterfully up and down our street, legs wide and with a slightly rolling gait, like a seaman on his deck.

Everyone was afraid of Red. So was I. I knew he carried a heavy metal knuckle-duster in his pocket.

I wanted to conquer my fear of Red. So I wrote a poem about him. This was my first piece of journalism in verse. By the next day the whole street knew it by heart and exulted with triumphant hatred.

One morning on my way to school, I suddenly came upon Red and his lieutenants. His eyes seemed to bore through me. 'Ah, the poet,' he drawled, smiling crookedly. 'So you write verses. Do they rhyme?'

Red's hand darted into his pocket and came out armed with its knuckle-duster; it flashed like lightning and struck my head. I fell down streaming with blood and lost consciousness.

This was my first remuneration as a poet. I spent several days in bed.

When I went out, with my head still bandaged, I again saw Red. I struggled with myself, but lost and took to my heels. At home I rolled on my bed, biting my pillow and pounding it in shame and impotent fury at my cowardice.

I made up my mind to vanquish it at whatever cost. I went into training at parallel bars and weights. After every session I would feel my muscles; they were getting bigger, but slowly. Then I remembered something I had read in a book about a miraculous Japanese method of wrestling which gave an advantage to the weak over the strong. I exchanged a week's ration card for a text book on ju-jitsu. For three weeks I stayed at home, practising with two other boys. Then I went out.

Red was sitting on the lawn in our yard, playing 'vingt-et-un' with his lieutenants. He was absorbed in the game.

Fear was still in me, urging me to go back. But I went up to the players and kicked and scattered the cards.

Red looked up, surprised at my impudence after my recent fight.

He got up slowly. 'You looking for more?' he asked menacingly.

As before, his hand dived into his pocket for the knuckle-duster. But I made a quick jabbing movement and Red, howling with pain, rolled on the ground. Bewildered, he got up and came at me, swinging his head furiously from side to side like a maddened bull.

I caught his wrist and squeezed slowly, as I had read in the book, until the knuckle-duster dropped from his limp fingers. Nursing his hand, Red fell down again. He was sobbing and smearing the tears over his pock-marked face with his grubby fist.

That day Red ceased to be the monarch of our street. And from that day on I knew for certain that one need not fear the strong. All one needs is to know the way to beat them. For every strong man there is a special ju-jitsu. What I learned also on this occasion was that to be a poet, I had not only to write poems, but know how to stand up for them.

Reader 4 **The Disciples Realize the Triumph of Jesus over Evil and Death.**
Luke 24: 13–35.

Song   Lord of the Dance (or Record).

Leader   Our prayer is an affirmation of the lordship of Christ.

Voice A Christ is the Lord of the smallest atom,

Voice B Christ is the Lord of outer space,

Voice C Christ is the Lord of the constellations,

79

Voices A Christ is the Lord of every place;
  B & C

Voice A Of the furthest star,

Voice B Of the coffee bar,

Voice C Of the length of the Berlin Wall,

Voice A Of the village green,

Voice B Of the Asian scene,

Voices A Christ is the Lord of all;
  B & C

Voice A Christ is the Lord of the human heart-beat,

Voice B Christ is the Lord of every breath,

Voice C Christ is the Lord of a man's existence,

Voices A Christ is the Lord of life and death;
  B & C

Voice A Christ is the Lord of our thoughts and feelings,

Voice B Christ is the Lord of all we plan,

Voice C Christ is the Lord of a man's decision,

Voices A Christ is the Lord of total man;
  B & C

Voice A In the local street,

Voice B Where people meet,

Voice C In the church or nearby hall,

Voice A In the factory,

Voice B In the family,

Voices A Christ is the Lord of all;
B & C

Voice A   Christ is the Lord of our love and courtship,

Voice B   Christ is the Lord of man and wife,

Voice C   Christ is the Lord of the things we care for,

Voices A Christ is the Lord of all our life.
B & C

Record   Hallelujah Chorus.
           During this record, the assembly disperses.

(e) The liberation of love

Voice   God loved the world so much that he gave his only Son, that everyone who
           has faith in him may not die but have eternal life.

Hymn   Ride on, ride on in majesty.

Leader   Through two readings, we shall think about the liberty which God's love
           brings to us. The first reading is from a children's story about a little
           prince who visits various planets and meets all sorts of people. In this
           extract, the prince meets a business man who is much concerned with his
           possessions, which he describes as 'matters of consequence'.

Reader 1 The fourth planet belonged to a businessman. This man was so much
           occupied that he did not even raise his head at the little prince's arrival.
           'Good morning', the little prince said to him. 'Your cigarette has gone out.'
           'Three and two make five. Five and seven make twelve. Twelve and
           three make fifteen. Good morning. Fifteen and seven make twenty-two.
           Twenty-two and six make twenty-eight. I haven't time to light it again.
           Twenty-six and five make thirty-one. Phew! Then that makes five-
           hundred-and-one million, six-hundred-twenty-two thousand, seven-hun-
           dred-thirty-one.'
           'Five hundred million what?' asked the little prince.

'Eh? Are you still there? Five-hundred-and-one million—I can't stop . . .
I have so much to do! I am concerned with matters of consequence. I don't
amuse myself with balderdash. Two and five make seven . . .'

'Five-hundred-and-one million what?' repeated the little prince, who
never in his life had let go of a question once he had asked it.

The businessman raised his head.

'During the fifty-four years that I have inhabited this planet, I have been
disturbed only three times. The first time was twenty-eight years ago,
when some giddy goose fell from goodness knows where. He made the most
frightful noise that resounded all over the place, and I made four mistakes
in my addition. The second time, eleven years ago, I was disturbed by an
attack of rheumatism. I don't get enough exercise. I have no time for loaf-
ing. The third time—well, this is it! I was saying, then, five-hundred-and-
one million—'

'Millions of what?'

The businessman suddenly realized that there was no hope of being left in
peace until he answered this question.

'Millions of those little objects,' he said, 'which one sometimes sees in the
sky.'

'Flies?'

'Oh, no. Little glittering objects.'

'Bees?'

'Oh, no. Little golden objects that set lazy men to idle dreaming. As for
me, I am concerned with matters of consequence. There is no time for
idle dreaming in my life.'

'Ah! You mean the stars?'

'Yes, that's it. The stars.'

'And what do you do with five-hundred millions of stars?'

'Five-hundred-and-one million, six-hundred-twenty-two thousand, seven-
hundred-thirty-one. I am concerned with matters of consequence: I am
accurate.'

'And what do you do with these stars?'

'What do I do with them?'

'Yes.'

'Nothing. I own them.'

'You own the stars? How is it possible for one to own the stars?'

'To whom do they belong?' the businessman retorted, peevishly.

'I don't know. To nobody.'

'Then they belong to me, because I was the first person to think of it.'

'Is that all that is necessary?'

'Certainly. When you find a diamond that belongs to nobody, it is yours.

When you discover an island that belongs to nobody, it is yours. When you get an idea before anyone else, you take out a patent on it: it is yours. So with me: I own the stars, because nobody else before me ever thought of owning them.'

'Yes, that is true,' said the little prince. 'And what do you do with them?'

'I administer them,' replied the businessman. 'I count them and recount them. It is difficult. But I am a man who is naturally interested in matters of consequence.'

The little prince was still not satisfied.

'If I owned a silk scarf,' he said, 'I could put it around my neck and take it away with me. If I owned a flower, I could pluck that flower and take it away with me. But you cannot pluck the stars from heaven . . .'

'No. But I can put them in the bank.'

'Whatever does that mean?'

'That means that I write the number of my stars on a little paper. And then I put this paper in a drawer and lock it with a key.'

'And that is all?'

'That is enough,' said the businessman.

Reader 2 **Christ Looked at the People.**

Christ looked at the people,
He saw them assailed by fear.
He saw the locked door,
He saw the knife in the hand,
He saw the buried coin,
He saw the unworn coat,
consumed by moth.
He saw the stagnant water
drawn and kept in the pitcher,
the musty bread in the bin,
the defended,
the unshared,
the ungiven.

He told them then,
of the love that casts out fear.
Of the love that is four walls
and a roof over the head.
Of the knife in the sheath,
of the coin in the open hand,
of the coat given

warm with the giver's life.
Of the water poured in the cup,
of the table spread.
The undefended,
the shared, the given,
the kingdom of Heaven.

Hymn   Crown him upon the throne.

Leader   Let us pray.

Lord, your love has shown us true freedom
    freedom from fear
            from selfishness
            from greed
            from jealousy.
Help us to understand the power of your love
    the power of sharing
            giving
            and caring.
Fill our lives with your love that, caring for others,
we may share with them, the liberty which you have brought us.

Amen.

Sources:
The poem on pages 72–73 is by Robert Herrick.
The Voices on pages 73–74 are from R. Hearn (compiler), *Modern Psalms by Boys*, University of London Press.
The reading on page 74, Reader 2 on pages 75–76, and Readers 2 and 3 on pages 77–79 are from Yevtushenko, *A Precocious Biography*, Collins.
Reader 1 on page 77 is from Richard Church, *Over the Bridge*, Heinemann.
The reading on pages 81–83 is from Antoine de Saint-Exupery, *The Little Prince*, Heinemann.
The poem on pages 83–84 is by Caryll Houselander, and published by Sheed and Ward.

7 WHITSUN
(GOD IN ACTION IN HUMAN LIFE)

(a) The fight for freedom

The aim of the following five assemblies is to show the spirit of God at work in the world, sometimes active through one man, sometimes through groups of men.

Hymn   Thy kingdom come.

Leader   Today we shall think about the beginning of a movement for freedom and justice in our own time. For the main part of our assembly, we shall listen to a speech by Dr. Martin Luther King, describing the beginning of his work in the movement to improve conditions for negroes in the United States. The movement began with a bus boycott in Montgomery, Alabama, in the United States. (Point out Alabama on a previously displayed map.) During the boycott every negro in Montgomery refused to ride on the buses for over a year, as a protest against the discrimination against negroes over seats, which was practised on the buses. At the end of this very remarkable protest, the negroes won their fight, and discrimination on the buses of Montgomery was finally ended. In this speech Dr. King urges negroes to stick together in their fight. Although he speaks in a language which we wouldn't use, nevertheless, he tells us of God's Spirit in the world, calling all men to stand up for justice, truth and freedom.

Record   Dr. King's entrance into the Civil Rights Movement. (If this is not possible, arrange for a reader to read it.)

Reader   'One day after finishing school, I was called to a little church down in Montgomery, Alabama. I started preaching there. Things were going well in that church. It was a marvellous experience, but one day a year later a lady by the name of Rosa Parks decided that she wasn't going to take it any longer. She stayed on a bus seat. You may not remember it because it is way back now several years, but it was the beginning of a Movement—

85

where 50,000 black men and women refused absolutely to ride the city 'buses and we walked together for 381 days. That's what we've got to learn in the north. The negroes have to learn to stick together. We stuck together: when we sent out the call, no negro rode the buses. It was one of the most amazing things I have ever seen in my life. The people of Montgomery asked me to serve as the spokesman and, as the President of the new organization (The Montgomery Improvement Association) came into being, to lead the boycott. I couldn't say no. Then we started our struggle together.

Things were going well for the first few days, but then about ten or fifteen days later, after the white people in Montgomery knew that we meant business, they started doing some nasty things. They started making nasty telephone calls and it came to the point that some days more than 40 telephone calls would come in, threatening my life, the life of my family, the life of my children. I took it for a while in a strong manner, but I never will forget one night very late. It was around midnight and you can have some strange experiences at midnight. I had been out meeting with the Steering Committee all that night and I came home. My wife was in bed and I immediately crawled into bed to get some rest, to get up early the next morning to try to keep things going, and immediately the telephone started ringing and I picked it up. On the other end was an ugly voice. That voice said to me in substance, "Nigger, we are tired of you and your mess now, and if you aren't out of this town in three days, we are going to blow your brains out and blow up your house." I had heard these things before, but for some reason that night it got to me and I turned over and I tried to go to sleep, but I couldn't sleep. I was frustrated, bewildered. Then I got up and went back to the kitchen and I started warming some coffee, thinking that coffee would give me a little relief. I got to the point when I couldn't take it any longer. I was weak. Something said to me, "You can't call on Daddy now—he's up in Atlanta 175 miles away. You can't even call on Mamma now. You've got to call on that something and that person your Daddy used to tell you about. That Power that can make a way out of no way." I discovered then that religion had to become real to me and I had to know God for myself. I bowed down over that cup of coffee, I never will forget it. Oh yes, I prayed a prayer and I prayed out loud that night. I said, "Lord, I am down here trying to do what is right. I think I am right, I think the cause that we represent is right, but Lord, I must confess that I am weak now. I am faltering. I am losing my courage." It seemed to me at that moment that I could hear an inner voice saying to me, "Martin Luther, stand up for righteousness. Stand up for justice. Stand up for truth. And lo, I will be with you, even until the end of the world."

Sometimes I feel discouraged. I don't mind telling you this morning, that sometimes I feel discouraged. I felt discouraged in Chicago. As I move through Mississippi and Georgia and Alabama I feel discouraged. Living every day under the threat of death, I feel discouraged sometimes. Living every day under extensive criticisms, even from negroes, I feel discouraged sometimes. Yes, sometimes I feel discouraged and feel my work is in vain, but then the Holy Spirit revives my soul again. "There is a balm in Gilead to make the wounded whole; there is a balm in Gilead to heal the sin-sick soul." God bless you.'

Leader   Prayers.

Lord, when you challenge us and show us inequality in your world,

Response Help us to stand up for justice.

Leader   When you challenge us and show us evil in your world,

Response Help us to stand up for righteousness.

Leader   When you challenge us and show us falseness in your world,

Response Help us to stand up for truth.

Song   We shall overcome.

All   May the grace of our Lord Jesus Christ
           and the love of God
           and the fellowship of the Holy Spirit
           be with us now and always.
                                    Amen.

(b) Youth in protest

Record   If I had a hammer.

Reader 1 And it shall come to pass afterward, that I will pour out my spirit on all flesh; your sons and your daughters shall prophesy; your old men shall dream dreams, and your young men shall see visions (Joel 2:28).

87

Leader   The following readings are all clips from newspapers giving accounts of activities by young people all of whom have spent time, energy and thought in an attempt to say something which they felt needed to be said. The first two of these readings report the activities of the Youth Delegation at the Fourth Assembly of the World Council of Churches held in Sweden in 1968.

Reader 1 **Youth Urge Positive Action to Close Rich-Poor Nations Gap** (Uppsala, July 10). The Fourth Assembly of the World Council of Churches 'will fail' if it does not place at the top of its agenda a programme of positive action to close the gap between rich and poor nations, a group of youth participants said here today.

Jan Pronk, a research associate of the Netherlands School of Economics, called for specific Assembly action to promote development in poor nations. He suggested churches urge individual self-taxation and call on their members to engage actively in the political life of their countries.

Reader 2 **Assembly Youth Condemn War in Vietnam** (Uppsala, July 8). A forceful resolution against the fighting in Vietnam was passed here today by youth participants at the Fourth Assembly of the World Council of Churches in a special youth plenary session held apart from the Assembly programme. The young people called for 'immediate cessation of bombing in all parts of Vietnam and for withdrawal of all non-indigenous military resources and personnel'. They declared that 'any political solution must involve all parties of the people's Vietnam. Any other involvement by nations must be decided by the United Nations.'

Reader 3 **Youth Urge New Way Of Thinking About Education.**
An overwhelming majority of young people at an International Youth Conference in Germany passed a resolution which argued for a new dimension in education. Feeling that one of the most important issues of today is that of world hunger and the struggle for economic justice, their resolution suggests that we need to educate young people not simply to live and work in their own country, but indeed to live in the world of international citizens. The development of 'International Man', they argue, is the goal of education. 'International Man' is not concerned only with the advancement of his own country, but more with the awareness of the needs of others throughout the world and his responsibility to others as a world citizen. Among the practical suggestions contained in the resolution are:

that students should study at least one language and culture other than their own,

that human conditions in the world must be seen as subject matter to be taught in schools,

that teachers should exchange with teachers of other cultures, so that on their return to their own country, they may share this international experience with others.

It was agreed that this resolution should be sent to the appropriate Government departments of the nations represented at the conference, to church boards and to departments of education. (Duisburg 1967).

Hymn   Rise up, O men of God.

Prayers Lord, we give thanks
        that we have been born into this world at this time
        that we have youth, energy and strength;
        that you have given us a vision of a world free from war,
                              hunger and selfishness.
    Help us to keep our visions before us
      and use our anger, our strength and our energy
    To fight and work unceasingly
      so that your kingdom may come on earth.
                        Amen.

(c) Youth in action

Record   Blowin' in the wind.

Reader   Ephesians 6: 10–18.

Leader   Yesterday we considered cuttings from newspapers and journals which showed young people speaking out about the problems and injustices of the world. Today's readings are also newspaper stories, this time showing young people taking positive action to meet the needs of others.

Every year thousands of young people try to help others in the community by taking part in a work camp. Here is a story of a group of girls from Great Britain and Germany.

Reader 1 Girls help the old folk. A group of teenage girls have swapped their school text books for washing-up towels, aprons and brooms and gone into Worthing old people's homes to share the work.

Entirely voluntarily, the girls, fifteen of them, have given up their mornings for the past nine days to do a real service for the older and less able. Aged sixteen to eighteen, the girls are at a work camp and are bunking down in the Baptist Church Hall in Christchurch Road, Worthing. In the party are eight girls from West Germany, members of a Protestant Mädchenwerk. Their offer to give a hand in looking after some of the town's elderly was snapped up by such organizations as the Council of Social Services' Ashmount and Caer Gwent homes, Gifford House (the home for disabled ex-Servicemen), Milton House (for the blind), and the West Sussex County Council homes Fairfield, Normanton and Sussex Lodge, Lancing.

Matron Deirdrie Dryden, at Ashmount, had this to say about her sixteen-year-old helper, Marie-Louise Schill, from West Germany: 'She has been most useful to us and the ladies love her. We'll be very sorry to lose her, although we have only had her for nine days. The residents just love having young people about.'

Leader   We frequently read in the press of young people going on a sponsored walk for a particular charity. Our second reading describes some of these activities. In this case, it was 'Shelter'. It might have been Oxfam, the handicapped, or something else.

Reader 2 Some boys from Malvern College, Worcester, went to a meeting in Coventry. The subject was 'Shelter', and they decided they must help. They returned to the College and persuaded their Headmaster to invite the speaker to talk to the school. Just before Easter the boys heard the talk, then went home armed with sponsor forms for a 30-mile walk they had organized. They got to work again, and between them urged 4,000 friends and relations to sponsor every mile they walked.

Three hundred and eighty boys took part in the walk, and £6,000 was sent to 'Shelter' to re-house families living in appalling conditions.

Prayer   We thank you, Lord
      that in the challenges of this world, we can serve you;
      that in seeing the needs of others, we can recognize our own good fortune;
      that in working for the good of others, we can find great companionship
           in our fellow-workers, we can discover more about themselves and
           their needs, more about ourselves and our needs, more about you
           and the kind of world you would have us live in.

For all that you give us we offer thanks.
Help us to turn our thanks into actions so that we can know and
serve you better.
Amen.

Hymn   Who would true valour see.

(d) The great agitation

Hymn   Eternal Ruler of the ceaseless round.

Reader 1 Intelligent school-leaver, boy or girl, required to train, with good pay, for interesting work in modern engineering firm. Excellent prospects. Five day week. Full details from Raws Limited, New Street, W.15.

Leader   Advertisements, similar to that are frequently found in the 'Situations Vacant' columns of our newspapers. But working conditions were not always like this. Less than 150 years ago, the working man could certainly not expect training, good working conditions and pay, excellent prospects and a five day week. In today's assembly we shall think about the beginnings of the Trade Union Movement in this country. The movement was born out of a vision of freedom, justice and the dignity of man. And its birth brought suffering to its early pioneers. The setting for its beginning is found in the village of Tolpuddle, Dorset.

Voice A 1830. Farmlabourer's wage, nine shillings a week.

Voice B 1832. Farmlabourer's wage, eight shillings a week.

Voice C 1833. Farmlabourer's wage, seven shillings a week.

Voice D 1834. Threat to reduce labourers' wages to six shillings a week.

Reader 2 At this time in Tolpuddle, there was a man of outstanding character, George Loveless, and under his leadership, some of the men of the village considered together how they might defend themselves against these progressive reductions of their wages.

Reader 3 The Tolpuddle men turned for advice and help to the Grand National Consolidated Trades Union. Two delegates of the Union came to Tolpuddle and as a result the Friendly Society of Agricultural Labourers was formed by the men.

Reader 4 The employers and magistrates in Tolpuddle were greatly alarmed that a trade union should be formed in the village. They feared that the result would be riots and other disturbances. One of the magistrates wrote to the Home Secretary for guidance about what to do. The result was that

Voice A 24th February, 1834, George Loveless and five of his fellow labourers arrested.

Voice B March 1834, Dorchester Assizes, George Loveless, James Loveless, James Hammett, Thomas Standfield, John Standfield, James Brine sentenced to seven years transportation.

Reader 1 Shortly afterwards, when the men were transported, they had hard and harrowing experiences overseas. They worked in chain gangs, in penal settlements and on farms, where their status was little, if any better than slaves. James Hammett said he was 'Sold like a slave for £1'.

Reader 2 At home agitation in the cause of the men and their families, grew and grew.

Voice A 24th March, 1834. Grand Meeting of the Working Classes—attended by over 10,000 people.

Voice B April 1834. Demonstration of more than 30,000 people in London.

Voice C The numbers of signatures on petitions for the men's release rose to over 800,000.

Voice D Continuous agitation and protest maintained during 1836 until finally in March 1836 the Home Secretary agreed to a full and free pardon for all the men.

Leader The Trade Union Movement, as we know it today, with its work and concern for the safety, health and well-being of all workers, grew out of the vision of freedom and dignity which these men had, the vision which they obeyed and for which they were prepared to suffer.

Reader 1 Man is most truly himself when he is panting after a dream, after a promise, after the cloud-cuckooland of his creative imagination. He loses himself, is already lost, when he feels such a journey is no longer necessary, when he thinks he has arrived.

Leader When he left the Court after his conviction, George Loveless threw to the crowd a paper on which were written some verses. He did not claim to have written them but they were verses which were sung at meetings during the campaign for the release of the Martyrs of Tolpuddle. We shall end this assembly by listening to them.

Reader 2 God is our Guide! From field, from wave,
From plough, from anvil and from loom,
We came our country's rights to save,
And speak the tyrant faction's doom;
    We raise the watchword 'Liberty'
    We will, we will, we will be free!

God is our Guide! No swords we draw,
We kindle not war's battle fires,
By reason, union, justice, law,
We claim the birthright of our sires;
    We raise the watchword 'Liberty'
    We will, we will, we will be free!

(e) 'Money back if not satisfied'

Leader Today, as we think of how people respond to challenges in today's world, we shall think about the actions of some Christians in Holland.

Reader 1 In 1967 in Holland it was announced that the tax system was to be re-assessed as under the previous system some people were paying an unfair amount of tax. The changes in the tax system meant that a number of people would receive a refund of money from the government. Most people were of course rather pleased about this, but a group of Christians who were very concerned about the poverty and hunger in the world decided to demonstrate *against* being given their money back. They argued as follows:

Voice A We are citizens of Holland and we should obey the laws of Holland.

Voice B But we are also citizens of the world.

Voice C A world where there is poverty and disease and hunger.

Voice D Two thirds of the world's people do not have enough to eat.

Voice A The laws of Holland mean that we shall have a refund of tax from the government and have a little more money to spend on ourselves.

Voice B But is there not also a law for the citizens of the world?

Voice C As citizens of the world we should care for our neighbour in other countries.

Voice D Surely this is a law which binds us all.

Voice A It is right for us to obey the laws of Holland.

Voice B But can it be right for us to obey the laws of Holland and become richer, while our neighbours in the world become poorer? If we do, surely we shall be ignoring the law 'Love your neighbour'.

Voice C 'Love your neighbour' is a world law and it is higher and more important than the laws of our own country.

Voice D We must therefore disobey the law of our own country. We must give the money back to our government, so that it can be used to feed the hungry. In this way, we shall obey the world law instructing us to love our neighbour.

Reader 1 These people, who belonged to a group called 'Shalom' (the word Shalom means peace and the group is an ecumenical work group which is especially concerned with political and social affairs in the world) then wrote the following letter to the Dutch Minister of Finance.

Reader 2 Your Excellency,   Holland, 1st July, 1967.
Today there will again be a decrease of tax in our country. The decision to do this is entirely according to the Dutch law and according to the democratic rules in our country. It is also according to these rules that each year the amount which should be given towards under-developed countries is budgeted for. Nationally speaking, this is all in good order.
Today and every day 10,000 are starving. Financial aid and trade with the developed countries is still not sufficient to reduce the great difference in the standard of living between the poor and the rich countries. This state of affairs is completely contrary to the basic law of human life. It mocks

the Universal Declaration of Human Rights. In world affairs in this matter, there is the greatest chaos.

A moral world law orders us to respect everybody's life and this implies a strong battle against hunger and injustice. Thus it forbids us to recognize the national law of increasing our standard of living and self-centredness. Therefore based on this moral world law, we have decided to declare the national law illegal and henceforth we send back to you the money received through this tax decrease—the amount with which, otherwise our salaries would have been increased. We will do this personally during a demonstration on Saturday, 1st July, in the Hague and from then onwards by cheque addressed to you and on which will be mentioned 'Money back if not satisfied.'

We will do this until our country faces up to its world tasks, by spending at least 2 per cent of the National Income for the under-developed countries and therefore makes its contribution to the reassessment of how incomes and resources are distributed throughout the world.

We should like to make clear that this action is not merely one of charity (one of the many and inadequate collections of money) but it is a political one. Its significance is that it points to the direction of placing world law above national law, so that our world will be inhabitable for everybody.

Reader 1 The Secretary of Shalom, Piet Reckman, said in a press interview,

Reader 3 You may comment that to be successful in our demonstration, we have to have the majority supporting us. We already have it. Two thirds of the world's population supports us.

Hymn Thy kingdom come, on bended knee.

Reader 1 Concerning Human rights, U Thant, General Secretary of the United Nations has said,

Reader 2 . . . The world now possesses the machinery and the resources to provide the higher standards of living to which the peoples of the developing countries aspire. What is still lacking, it seems to me, is the will and the vision to undertake a broad and bold programme which would cut across national boundaries and ideological barriers and unite us in a common effort to improve the lot of two thirds of mankind.

Leader Let us pray.
Lord, your world is full of riches

95

Response Help us to share them.

Leader   Your world is full of problems

Response Help us to understand them.

Leader   Your world is full of challenges

Response Help us to respond in action.

Leader   Your world is full of selfishness and injustice

Response Help us to fight for what is right.

Leader   Lord, you have told us that your Spirit will guide us into all truth.

Response Help us to serve your Spirit in the world.

Amen.

Sources:

Readers 1 and 2 on page 88 are from Ecumenical Press Service Clips.

Reader 1 on pages 89–90 is from the *Brighton Evening Argus*, August 1967.

The Service on pages 91–93 is based on material supplied by the Trades Unions Congress.

Reader 1 at the foot of page 92 is from Werner Pelz, *Crowning Absurdity*.

The Service on pages 93–96 is based on material supplied by Trouw (Amsterdam) and translated by Rietge Onvlee.